$15.00

3280075101
2X-1

The Common Hangman

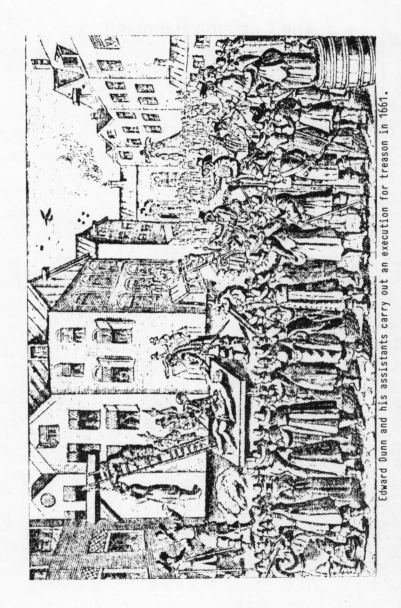

Edward Dunn and his assistants carry out an execution for treason in 1661.

THE COMMON HANGMAN

English and Scottish hangmen
before the abolition of
Public Executions

by

JAMES BLAND

IAN HENRY PUBLICATIONS
1984

ISBN 0 86025 884 X

Printed by Whitstable Litho Ltd.,
for Ian Henry Publications Ltd.,
38 Parkstone Avenue, Hornchurch, Essex RM11 3LW

CONTENTS

Introduction

For over 800 years, beginning in the reign of Henry I, the death penalty remained constantly in force in Britain. For the greater part of that period one could be executed for any one of a large number of offences, some of which were fairly trivial. Governments of those days could conceive of no other means of maintaining the peace.

The hangman was thus a familiar figure in many towns and cities, carrying out his work in public, generally unmasked, and often before huge crowds. His indispensability was taken for granted, his place in society unassailable. He was the most important instrument of the criminal law.

Though primarily an executioner, he was often expected to inflict public whippings as well. In some towns, where few executions took place, he probably did little else. But in London he had a whole range of lesser punishments to inflict, in addition to hanging a great many people every year. He was also expected, in cases of treason, to carry out more frightful types of execution.

The post could therefore be dangerous as well as demanding, particularly during periods of political or religious persecution. It is therefore not surprising to learn that he sometimes had to be guarded for his own safety. But the hangman was also a great entertainer. The excitement generated by public executions was often both widespread and pleasurable, affecting people of all classes - the respectable as well as the rabble.

On many occasions a festive spirit prevailed, with street vendors doing a brisk trade among the crowds. At Tyburn galleries were erected to provide seats for anyone willing to pay for them. There were also rooms which could be hired in houses overlooking the scene. Later, special excursion trains enabled large numbers of people to travel great distances to watch executions in provincial towns.

There were, it is true, many outrages committed by the spectators. When the condemned was a popular hero, like the jail-breaker Jack Sheppard, or a pathetic individual who had everybody's sympathy, a riot might take place. When it was feared that the body would be taken for dissection, an attempt might be made to prevent this happening. But the significant thing about these outrages is that they usually took place after an execution. There were very few attempts made to rescue the condemned.

Executions gave the populace the same intensity of experience as certain sporting fixtures and, however sympathetic they might have been towards the prisoners, they rarely had any wish to prevent them being carried out. A last-minute reprieve could be greeted with jubilation by the mob - but it could just as easily lead to rioting.

The hangman - in the cities, at any rate - had many admirers. Sometimes after an execution he would be treated and could sell pieces of his ropes as souvenirs. The rope with which a famous or notorious criminal had been hanged could be sold by the inch, bringing in a lot of money. Other items connected with the criminal, such as his clothes, might also be bought from the hangman.

His other tasks - whipping, branding, mutilation or exposure in the pillory - gave entertainment too, though they did not normally draw such large crowds. Even so, if a whipping was inflicted to the satisfaction of the spectators, a collection might be taken on the hangman's behalf.

The hangman, then, served both the government and the populace at the same time, meeting the demands of justice on the one hand and the need for excitement on the other. But he did not have the respectability of the legislators and judges who gave him work and he was not always popular even with the crowds who gathered to watch the sufferings of his victims. There was, in fact, a stigma upon his post and all who occupied it; for it was, by common consent, a revolting way of earning a living.

Most people, it seems, felt a strong need to absolve themselves of any personal responsibility for the deaths of others, particularly when the offence committed was a minor one. We find, for example, that an increase in the number of capital offences during the late seventeenth and early eighteenth centuries led to a practice among juries of convicting offenders only of non-capital crimes. While it was a capital offence to steal from a dwelling-house to the value of forty shillings, they frequently under-valued stolen goods to make offenders guilty of stealing to the value of thirty-nine shillings; and, while it was a capital offence to steal from a shop to the value of five shillings, they just as often found them guilty of pilfering just four shillings and tenpence.

This practice, sometimes encouraged by judges, was taken to absurd lengths with the under-valuing of coins and banknotes.

We have no reason to suppose that the jurors concerned derived any less enjoyment from watching executions than anyone else: the need to disclaim personal involvement in the death of a petty offender was a strong enough motive for behaving as they did. No doubt it was the same need that so often caused the crowds to commit outrages after an execution had taken place and perhaps it was also this that caused society as a whole to ostracise the hangman.

Whatever the reason for it, there was a

marked reluctance on the part of respectable men to perform the hangman's duties. All too often, it seems, our sheriffs and magistrates had to employ ruffians and dissolutes, whose conduct at the place of execution was hardly awe-inspiring. The stigma upon the post could only be reinforced by such reprobates.

Of the individuals whose lives, characters and working conditions are the subject of this book, all held office – or at least officiated – in England or Scotland before public executions were abolished.

Biographical sketches of a few of them are to be found in *The Hangmen of England* (1929) by Horace Bleackley; three – Richard Brandon, Jack Ketch and William Calcraft – have entries in *The Dictionary of National Biography*. There is also a certain amount of information about some of the others to be found in works like *Tyburn Tree: its History and Annals* (1908) by Alfred Marks, *A History of Capital Punishment* (1932) by John Laurence, *The Domestic Annals of Scotland* (1858) by Robert Chambers, and in one or two local histories, miscellanies and journals. But that is about all.

It must also be said that some of the information published in some of these works has been derived from sources that are by no means reliable. Several writers in the field of 'popular antiquities' have given credence to 'curious facts' about hangmen which, in the interests of accuracy, ought to have been discarded.

This may be seen as understandable in view of the paucity of research materials available. Unlike some of our modern hangmen, those of earlier times left us no diaries or autobiographies; no *Memoirs of J Ketch* have been unearthed. The chronicles, broadsides and newspapers of those times contain many references to 'the common hangman' or 'the executioner', but tell us remarkably little about him as an individual. As for official records, these, in many cases, do not even mention him. However, this is hardly a justification for using uncorroborated 'evidence' from ballads and poems as historical fact.

For the purposes of this book, most of the sources used by the above writers have been consulted, as have many unknown to them. Fresh information - albeit in small items - has come to light about most of the hangmen concerned and also about other members of the same profession. Everything of doubtful authenticity has been either discarded or questioned.

Our hangmen were important enough to be worthy of such attention, even if the writers of their own times thought otherwise.

Guy Fawkes and his fellow conspirators executed by Derrick and his assistants.

Early Hangmen

Many hangmen of the late Middle Ages were men in bondage, the execution of felons being imposed upon them by their conditions of tenure.

Thomas Blount's *Fragmenta Antiquitatis.* for example, tells us that in the Manor of Stoneley, Warwickshire, "there were anciently four bondmen, whereof each held one messuage and one *Quartron* of land, by the service of *making* the *Gallows* and *hanging* the *Thieves*" Each was obliged "to plow, reap, make the lord's malt, and do other servile work", and to wear a red clout on his upper garment in order that he might be recognised as a hangman.

That there were regional variations in the use of such men is seen by comparing this example with an entry in the *Calendar of the Patent Rolls* for 29th March, 1446, which reads:

"Grant to the king's bondmen of the counties of Caernarvan, M[er]yonnyth and Anglesey in North Wales, that they be quit of the hanging and execution of all felons in the said counties, in consideration of their petition shewing that they are compelled herein by the sheriffs, by reason whereof bondmen have with drawn from the said counties to divers parts of England, so that many towns are desolate and divers rents, services and pence taken away; though in the county of Flynt the sheriffs do such execution before the justices."

Later, in Tudor times, we find that "John Croxton de Ravenscroft, gent., held certain lands and tenements, with the appurtenances, in Kinderton, of Thomas Venables, lord of that manor, by service(*inter alia*) to find for the said Thomas Venables and his heirs one hangman, to hang murderers and felons within the manor when required." It is known that the John Croxton in question rendered this service in 1581 by hiring a John Lingard to hang a murderer named Hugh Stringer.

In the towns, it seems, the work of the hangman was sometimes done by holders of other posts; the porter of the City of Canterbury during the reigns of Henry II and Henry III was also executioner for the whole of Kent, for which he had an allowance from the Sheriff of twenty shillings a year.

In some cases, however, we find that the onus of carrying out an execution - or finding someone else to carry it out - was upon the criminal's prosecutor, who was often the victim of the crime. In Preston, for example, it was decided in the twelfth century that "[if] any be taken for robbery or other misdeed and adjudged to death, he who prosecutes shall carry out the judgment."

In Romney, as late as 1498, it became the rule that "if the pele (appellee) in playne hundred make any knowynge (acknowledgment or confession) of felony, be he condempnet, ande it is to wytte that the bayleff shall fynd the gallowys and the rope, and the suter which maketh the appele shall fynde the hangman. And if he may fynde non hangman neither that he wyll noght do that same office himself, he shall dwelle in prison with the felon unto the time that he wyll do that office or else find an hangman."

There was a similar obligation upon prosecutors in some towns where different forms of execution were used - as in Dover, where it was laid down, also in the fifteenth century, that "all tho that shull suffer deth shall be lede to (and thrown from) a clyffe yealled Sharpenesse, and yf he be atteynte at the sute of the partye the appelour shall do execucioun, and if it be at the kyng's sute the baylly shall doo it."

It is probable, however, that some towns at this time had official hangmen, receiving regular salaries and fees; that these, unlike the porter at Canterbury, were <u>not</u> holders of other posts; and that they inflicted other forms of punishment as well as carrying out sentences of death.

It is likely that other towns had regular *unofficial* hangmen, paid for their work by the sheriff, the prosecutor, or whoever else would otherwise have had to carry out the execution himself.

The earliest London hangman of whom there is any record was named Cratwell or Gratnell. He was appointed to the post in 1534 and remained in it until his death four years later. It was not he who beheaded Anne Boleyn: the Calais executioner was brought to London to perform this particular duty. We may be sure, though, that he officiated on many other important occasions, as well as hanging many lesser offenders. He was described by Wriothesley as "a conninge butcher in quarteringe of men".

With two other malefactors, Cratwell was himself hanged on 1st September, 1538 (a Sunday) for "robbinge a bouth in Bartlemewe fayre", the executions being carried out in Clerkenwell, "where the wrestlinge is kept, after the wrestlinge was done... on a payre of gallowes, newe made." The chronicler, Edward Hall, who was present at the death, estimated that the executions were watched by a crowd of about 20,000 people.

We do not know who succeeded Cratwell or how long that person remained in office*, but Stephen Perlin, who witnessed the Duke of North-

---

*In 1541 we find that Margaret Pole, the elderly Countess of Salisbury, was executed on East Smithfield Green by a clumsy novice "who hideously hacked her neck and shoulders before the decapitation was accomplished." <u>D.N.B.</u> (ref. <u>Margaret Pole</u>)

umberland's execution on 22nd August, 1553, tells us that the individual who officiated then "was lame of a leg... and... wore a white apron, like a butcher."

This was clearly the same hangman who was hanged in 1556 – an event recorded in Machyn's*Diary:*

"The ij day of July rod in a care [rode in a cart] v. unto Tyborne: on was the hangman with the stump-lege for stheft [theft], wyche he had hangyd mony a man and quartered mony, and hed [beheaded] many a nobull man and odur [other]."

The London hangman was always the busiest; there were always more executions there than anywhere else in the country. It is therefore likely that he had had a regular official post since the twelfth century.†

Further variations in custom, which may have originated in the Middle Ages, become apparent from references to later hangmen which have come to light.

The claim that the hangman of York was usually a pardoned felon is not without substance, as the following report in the *Gentleman's Magazine* of 1731 shows:

"At the Assizes held at York the 3 following Malefactors receiv'd Sentence of Death, viz. Bemjamin [sic] Armitt, James Wood, and John Ward, Matthew Blackbourn capitally convicted at the same time, had his Pardon, being made Hangman. The 3 first were executed at Tybourn near York, March 29th."

The Taunton post was hereditary*; a Captain William LeGeyt, visiting the town in 1804, recorded that the office was held by 'a poor devil' named Joshua Otway, and had been in the same family since

† The death penalty was reintroduced in England by Henry I after being abolished by William I.

*There is a reference to hereditary hangmen in Coriolanus, and it is possible that many hereditary posts did exist in Shakespeare's time. However, we have no proof of this.

the Bloody Assizes of 1685.†

In Newcastle upon Tyne in 1705 Alexander Robinson was appointed hangman 'in the room of Thomas Cooper'. There had been a hanging there in 1701; there was not to be another until 1733. However, there was plenty of other work for him, for it was his duty 'to whip delinquents, and cut the houghs, or *sinews* of the houghs, of swine that were found infesting the streets of the town.' He was known locally as the *whipper and hougher* for this reason.

Scotland, like England, had many hangmen, though far fewer executions were carried out there.

The hangman of Edinburgh was sometimes called the *dempster* or *doomster* having the duty of pronouncing sentence upon criminals convicted of capital offences. Generally, though, he was called the *lockman* and it is assumed that this arose out of his privilege of taking a *lock* of meal out of every sack in the city market.

Other Scottish hangmen also had the duty of pronouncing sentences of death, and some of these are also referred to as the *dempster* in contemporary reports.

In Stirling in the seventeenth century the hang man was known as the *staffman* evidently because his appointment was marked by the presentation of a staff of office. One such hangman was appointed for life in 1633, his absence from the town being punishable by death, as this extract from the Burgh Records shows:

"20 May, 1633. - Thomas Grant, borne in Glenalmond, under David Murray of Bulhindye, ressavit and sworne servand and executionar to this town of Stirling his lyfe tyme, and sall not remove nor absent himself aff the toune, but license of the Magistrats,

†A copy of LeGeyt's journal, or part of it, is contained in unpublished notes on Taunton by L E J Brooke, held at the Local History Library at Taunton Castle.

under the pane of daithe."

John McClelland, a capital offender, was appointed hangman of Glasow on the same conditions in 1605. In this case, we learn, the provost, magistrates and council ordained that a fine would be imposed on anyone in the burgh who abused him, whether by word or by deed.

Clearly, they did not expect him to be popular.

If these varying methods of appointing the hang man originated in the Middle Ages, some of the perquisites appertaining to the post - for example, the right of many Scottish hangmen to levy market dues - almost certainly did so too. The London hangman's right to the clothes of his victims was recognised in Cratwell's time: it was for this reason that Sir Thomas More took off his gown of silk camlet and put on one of frieze before his execution. The Lieutenant of the Tower had advised him that such a gown would be good enough for the person who was to have it.

Father and Son

Of Derrick, who was hangman for the City of London and County of Middlesex at the beginning of the seventeenth century, little is known. It was he who beheaded the Earl of Essex in 1601; it was also he, in all likelihood, who executed Guy Fawkes and his fellow conspirators in 1606, but when he acceded to the post or how he came to leave it is also unknown.

A contemporary ballad has given rise to the belief that he had been in Cadiz under Essex in 1596. It is this, too, which suggests that while there he carried out 23 hangings, as well as being sentenced to death himself for rape. However, this can hardly be considered a reliable source when we have no corroborative evidence that he ever went to Cadiz.

We know, however, that he was still in office on 12th July, 1606, for on that day he was flogged in Bridewell (the house of correction) 'for not using a hot iron to brand a prisoner in Newgate the same morning'. He must therefore have held the post for at least five years.

Tyburn, by this time, was already established as the common place of execution; the triangular gallows known as the Triple Tree had been erected there in 1571. It was in regular use, generally for multiple executions: it has been estimated that during the first ten years of James I's reign no fewer than 1,472 London and Middlesex prisoners were put to

death, almost all of them by hanging. In view of the
enormous crowds that used to gather at Tyburn and
the many people who were whipped 'at the cart's
tail', it is safe to assume that Derrick was a well-
known character.

By 1611 the post was occupied by Gregory
Brandon, who was to continue as hangman for almost
thirty years, becoming even more well-known and
probably even more detested.

Brandon lived in Rosemary Lane, Whitechapel,
and had a wife named Alice. Early in 1611 he was
convicted of manslaughter following the death of a
Simon or Simeon Morton on or about 11th December
the previous year. The Middlesex Sessions records
show that he only managed to escape the gallows by
pleading benefit of clergy:

*"8 January, 8 James I (A.D.1610-11) Gregory
Brandon of London, yeoman, for assaulting Simon
Mooreton at Whitechapple and wounding him with 'a
hanger' [a short sword] so that he died. Guilty. No
goods. Seeks the book. Reads as a clerk. Branded
with the letter T [for Tyburn] and delivered
according to the form of the statute. Indicted of
homicide."**

Among the names of the witnesses we find
Alice Morton, Thomas Reynolds and Agnes Tanner.
The conviction and branding were not the end of the
matter, for on 22nd January the same year we find
the following recognisances recorded:

*"Gregory Brandon, of Rosemarilane (the hang-
man), John Williams, of the same, labourer, and John
Turner, of the same, 'fisher', for the same Gregory*

*The fact that Brandon was able to claim benefit of clergy
should not be taken as proof that he could read, for the test
was always the same (one only had to read, or pretend to read,
the first verse of the 51st Psalm) and many illiterates were
able to pass it with the help of the jailer. The branding, in
the left thumb, was inflicted to prevent laymen being able to
claim the privilege a second time.

to keep the peace towards Thomas Regnolds [*sic*], of Rosemarilane, barber-surgeon."

And on 16th September we find, also among the recognisances:

"Gregory Brandon of Rosemary Lane, yeoman, for Alice his wife, Alice Morton and Agnes Tanner, both of the same, widows, to keep the peace."

There are further references to both Brandon and his wife in the sessions records of 1615.

On 20th April we find that Robert Dewer, of Rosemary Lane, yeoman, was accused of stealing a 'counter-poynte', worth £20; and Emma Elliott, of the same, widow, of "receiving and helping him at the same after the said felony". Dewer was found not guilty; Emma was discharged without having to stand trial, the grand jury having decided that there was 'no true bill' in her case. The prosecutors are named as Henry Porter and Alice Brandon, neither of whom was the owner of the stolen property.

Then, on 18th May, we find that Gregory Brandon entered into a recognisance to give evidence against Thomas Nicholas, also of Rosemary Lane, sailor, for stealing three keys, a chain and a pair of gloves, the property of 'the said Gregory'.

Finally, at the sessions beginning on 29th November, William Clarke and Emma Elliott, of Rosemary Lane, and John Barnes, of Ratcliffe, sailor, were accused of stealing two carpets, various items of apparel, eleven pieces of pewter and a few other articles in a robbery in Rosemary Lane; and a James Foster or Forster and his wife Joan, together with Gregory Brandon and his wife, all of Rosemary Lane, were accused of "helping and receiving them after the said felony".

Clarke was "respited to the Gaol of Surrey because a burglary was done there and he wished to acknowledge to [it]". Emma Elliott was found guilty and sentenced to death. There was no 'true bill' against John Barnes or Joan Foster, but Barnes was "bound over to answer the said Gregory". James

Foster and Gregory Brandon were tried and acquitted, Brandon being "bound over to give evidence against the said John [Barnes]." Alice Brandon was recorded as being 'at large'.

We do not know the outcome of all this: there appear to be no further references to either Brandon or his wife in any of the sessions records; whatever happened, it did not bring the hangman's tenure of office to an end.

A year later Brandon had the distinction of being granted a coat of arms, as we discover in an entry in the *Calendar of State Papers (Domestic Series)*for January, 1617:

"*York Herald played a trick on Garter King-at-Arms, by sending him a coat of arms drawn up for Gregory Brandon, said to be a merchant of London, and well-descended, which Garter subscribed, and then found that Brandon was the hangman; Garter and York are both imprisoned, one for foolery, the other for knavery.*"

This information may not be entirely correct, for it appears from another source that the victim of the trick was not Garter but Clarenceaux King of Arms (the chronicler William Camden) and that it had been devised as a means of discrediting him because York was piqued by his promotion.

To the populace the details could hardly have mattered. The important thing was that the hangman had somehow been granted a coat of arms – a fact that undoubtedly caused much mirth among his neighbours in Whitechapel and many a grim jest at the gallows. It has been suggested that the title of *esquire* which was popularly given to later London hangmen, was a direct result of this, but we do not know whether this is really true.

Gregory Brandon continued as hangman well into the reign of Charles I. It is believed that he was assisted in his later years by his son Richard, who succeeded him about 1639, claiming the post (or so it was said) 'by inheritance'.

The number of executions was by this time considerably lower (though still substantial): during the whole 24 years of Charles' reign there were only 815 Middlesex prisoners executed, compared with 704 during the first 10 years of James I, and it is probable that the number of London prisoners executed fell similarly.

This reduction, of course, meant fewer fees and suits of clothes for the hangman, but is unlikely to have helped improve his public standing.

Richard Brandon was sometimes referred to by his contemporaries as 'Gregory' or 'Young Gregory'. He is known to have been married and appears to have lived in Rosemary Lane all his life. His entry in *The Dictionary of National Biography* tells us:

"In 1641 he was a prisoner in Newgate on a charge of bigamy, from which he seems to have cleared himself (The Organ's Eccho 1641)."

He was the executioner of the Earl of Strafford in 1641, Archbishop Laud in 1645, and the Earl of Holland, the Duke of Hamilton and Lord Capel in 1649. Some writers have also accepted that he was one of the two masked men at the execution of Charles I.

"On 15 Oct. 1660 William Hulett, or Howlett, was condemned to death for having been Charles's executioner; but three witnesses asserted positively that Brandon was the guilty person, and their state-ment is corroborated by three tracts, published at the time of Brandon's death", says the *D.N.B.* entry.

The value of this evidence has, however, been seriously questioned by J G Muddiman in his *Trial of King Charles the First* (1928). Brandon, on hearing that the King was to be put to death, had declared that he would not carry out the task. Attempts at bribery and intimidation were - initially, at least - to no avail. On 30th January, 1649, he was "fetched out of bed by a troop of horse" to perform the execution, but, for all we know, may still have persisted in his refusal. Muddiman's belief was that he had been kept under guard in order that he could be made to *appear* to have been the executioner.

Mary Brandon, the hangman's widow, was still alive at the time of Hulett's trial, but was not called as a witness, presumably because she was unwilling to state that her husband had officiated at the King's death.

Richard Brandon died on 20th June, 1649, his body being buried the following day in the churchyard of St Mary, Whitechapel. His interment was recorded as follows:

"21st. Rich. Brandon, a man out of Rosemary Lane."

And to this was later added a marginal note in a different hand:

"This R Brandon is supposed to have cut off the head of Charles the First."

The next hangman of London was William Low (or Loe or Lowen), "a dust carrier and cleaner of the dung hills". Nine days after the death of his predecessor he hanged 24 people at Tyburn (the largest number that could be 'comfortably' hanged there at a time, i.e., without the bodies touching those adjacent). He remained in office until his death on or about 12th August, 1653.

The Original Jack Ketch

By 1657 the post of hangman of London was occupied by a fellow named Edward Dunn, for the Middlesex Sessions Rolls record that on 7th October that year recognisances were entered into by and on behalf of a victualler who had been "taken the last Lord's Day in sermon tyme in the house of Edward Dunn executioner with three more notorious thieves some of them formerly burnt in the hand".

The house, 'near or in *Goldenlane*', Cripplegate, was evidently one of the meeting- places of a well-organised gang; it was said that about this time the hangman himself was apprehended and only narrowly avoided punishment.

Dunn was the executioner of the Regicides; it was also he who hanged the exhumed bodies of Cromwell, Ireton and Bradshaw on the gallows at Tyburn. He had a great relish for the shedding of blood and was not above taunting condemned men at the place of execution. On one occasion he visited a prisoner due to be drawn, hanged and quartered* the

*In the seventeenth century, the expression drawn, hanged and quartered was more commonly used than the alternative, in which the order of the first two words is reversed. This is because the word drawn, to be strictly accurate, signifies merely that the prisoner was conveyed to the place of execution on a hurdle or sledge rather than in the usual hanging-cart.

following day and demanded money "that he might be favourable to him" at his execution. He was, it seems, allowed some discretion in the matter of whether such prisoners should be cut down for disembowelment while still alive - as the sentence always directed - or left to hang until they were dead.

Dunn is known to have died on 11th September, 1663, but who succeeded him we do not know.

The next occupant of the post of whom we have any record was Jack Ketch, the most famous hangman of all.

****

The earliest known references to Ketch appear in tracts published in 1678. It is clear from these, however, that he was already an established figure by this time, so it is likely that his appointment had taken place some years previously. Some writers have assumed that he became hangman soon after Dunn's death.

At any rate, he held the office for most of the period 1678 to 1686 and at his death had such a shocking reputation for savagery and incompetence that his name became the traditional name for the hangman in many parts of the country and remained so until well into the nineteenth century.

Ketch - or Catch, as he was often called - was the executioner of the victims of the Popish Plot conspiracy in 1678-81, of those involved in the Rye House Plot of 1683, of the Duke of Monmouth in 1685, and of countless others. It was also he who whipped Titus Oates from Aldgate to Newgate on 20th May, 1685, and from Newgate to Tyburn two days later.

In a broadside published in 1680 he is referred to as "The Romanists best DOCTOR, who by one Infallible Remedy, Perfectly Cures all *Popish-Diseases* whatsoever in a Quarter of an Hours time, or Half an Hour at utmost, By an Approved *Dose* which never yet Failed His *Patients* ... A Small Dose whereof

being Rightly applyed... sends the *Patient* Bolt-
upright to *Heaven* in a *String* without Calling at *Purg-
atory* by the way..."

And in a poem published in 1685, Oates,
alluding to the 16 people he had sent to their deaths
(all but one of them innocent of the crimes for
which they suffered), is made to say:

> *The many famous deeds that I have done,*
>
> *Since the kingdom's mighty work begun,*
>
> *Have made* Ketch *half as rich as* Squire Dun.

Ketch's activities were not confined to London.
It is known that he carried out the execution of
Stephen College, the 'Protestant Joiner', who was
drawn, hanged and quartered in Oxford on 31st
August, 1681. He may even have accompanied Judge
Jeffreys on the Western Circuit [the Bloody Assizes]
after the suppression of Monmouth's revolt.

On 21st July, 1683, he beheaded Lord William
Russell on a scaffold in Lincoln's Inn Fields, having
first received his customary gratuity. Dr Gilbert
Burnet informs us that the prisoner's head was "cut
off at two strokes", while Sir Charles Lyttelton (who,
like Burnet, was a witness) maintains:

> *"The hangman gave him 3 blows, besides
> sawing with ye ax, before he cut his head of."*

Whichever is the more truthful of these
accounts, it was generally believed that the execution
had been bungled, and soon afterwards there appeared
a broadside, *The Apologie of John Ketch Esq.*,
apparently written by or on behalf of the hangman
himself in order to vindicate his performance - "since
it is not fit that so Publick a Person as the Executioner of Justice... should lye under the scandal of
untrue Reports, and be unjustly Expos'd to popular
Clamour..."

In it he denied having been drunk or in any
way to blame for the fact that more than one blow
had been necessary, claiming that "my Lord himself
was the real obstract that he had not a quicker
dispatch out of this World"; that the prisoner "did

not dispose him for recieving of the fatal Stroke in such a posture as was most suitable"; and that, having refused to be blindfolded or to give a signal to show that he was ready, he had "somewhat heav'd his Body" as the axe fell. The hangman added, as if for good measure:

"Moreover after having receiv'd the Guinnies, *and according to my duty ask't his Lordships Pardon; I receav'd some Interruption just as I was taking Aim and going to give the Blow."*

The statement did not succeed in putting a stop to the rumours of Ketch's incompetence.

Two years later the whipping of Titus Oates was carried out with the utmost severity in the presence of innumerable spectators. The historian Echard says:

"The first Day he was ty'd to a Cart, where he made hideous Bellowings, and sounded several Times with the greatness of the Anguish.

"The second Day, he was not able to go or stand; but this, Lestrange *tells us was because he had made himself scandalously drunk: However, he was then plac'd and dragg'd upon a Sledge, where he became a dismal and piteous Spectacle to the People, who cou'd much better judge of his Punishment, than his Crimes.*

"In sum, as he himself says, he sustain'd un-expressable Torments; *and his escaping with Life was insisted on by his Friends as something miraculous, and a signal Testimony of his Innocence."*

The 'piteous spectacle' was still fresh in the minds of the populace when, less than two months afterwards, Ketch was called upon to behead the Duke of Monmouth.

The execution took place on Tower Hill on 15th July, 1685. As at the execution of Russell, the block was low - that is to say, it was a block before which the victim had to lie full-length, rather than kneel. The scaffold, as always upon such occasions, was draped with black cloth.

"Here are six guineas for you," said Monmouth, handing Ketch the money. "Pray do your business well. Don't serve me as you did my Lord Russell. I have heard you struck him three or four times." He then turned to his servant, who accompanied him on the scaffold: "Here, take these remaining guineas and give them to him if he does his work well."

"I hope I shall," said Ketch.

"If you strike me twice, I cannot promise you not to stir," warned the prisoner. He lay on the floor of the scaffold and put his neck in place, then raised himself up on his elbow. "Prithee, let me feel the axe," he said to Ketch. And then, when he had felt the edge of the blade: "I fear it is not sharp enough." "It is sharp enough and heavy enough," insisted the hangman.

Monmouth put himself back into position in readiness to receive the blow. The crowd was silent, as indeed it had been almost from the moment of the prisoner's arrival; the only sounds were the pious utterances of four divines in attendance. Ketch raised the axe.

He was not as sure of himself as he had tried to appear; the reference to Russell's execution had evidently unnerved him. He must have been aware, too, that although the rebellion in the West Country had failed, Monmouth was still popular and many in the crowd regarded him as a hero. The result was that Ketch, in a distracted state of mind, brought down the axe too lightly and inflicted only a wound.

Monmouth raised his head and turned to look him in the face, as if to upbraid him, but prostrated himself again without a word. Ketch struck a second ineffectual blow and then, in desperation, a third. Then, to the horror of the dignitaries, the attendants and the crowd, he threw down the axe, crying: "God damn me, I can do no more! My heart fails me!"

The Sheriff of London and others on the scaffold forced him to take up the axe afresh and finish his work, but two further blows were needed and, even then (according to one acccount), he "severed not [the prisoner's] head from his body till he cut it off with his knife."

Finally, the executioner held up Monmouth's head - "but there was no shouting, but many cryed."

Afterwards, says Evelyn, the crowds were so incensed by the bungling "that had [Ketch] not ben guarded & got away they would have torne him in pieces."

****

Ketch, then, was notorious both for his brutality and for his incompetence - and this notoriety, says one writer, "was perpetuated by the natural application of his name to the executioner, who regularly figured in the puppet-show drama of 'Punchinello', introduced into England about this time from Italy and popularised by Robert Powell and others during the reign of Anne." He is still one of the characters in Punch and Judy shows even today.

We do not know how he came to be appointed to his post, or what occupation he had previously pursued; we do not know, either, if he had fallen foul of the law or been in any way associated with criminals.

His last address, given in his burial record, was Spread Eagle Alley, the location of which is given in Edward Hatton's *New View of London* (1708); it lay, says this authority, "on the N. side of *Bow Str.* near the S. end of *King Str. Westminster.*"

The burial entry also informs us that Jack (i.e., John) Ketch was his real name, rather than a corruption of Jacquet, as was once suggested.

In 1679 there appeared a tract, *The Man of Destiny's Hard Fortune* in which it was claimed that he had recently been imprisoned on suspicion of debt - "charged with two and twenty Pounds, and odd Farthings... for Milk" - and thus prevented from carrying out his duties at a time when "an opportunity for business under the most propitious Influences" existed.

It has also been claimed (apparently on the slenderest evidence) that in 1682 he "successfully struck for higher wages".

Some months after the execution of Monmouth – probably early in January, 1686 – he was removed from office and committed to Bridewell for "affronting the sheriffs of London", his place being taken by a Pascha Rose.

This man, according to Narcissus Luttrell, was a butcher, but an entry in the Middlesex Sessions Rolls describes him as a labourer. J G Muddiman, in *The Bloody Assizes* suggests that he had been employed as Ketch's assistant, but does not give any evidence of this.

Rose, at any rate, was in trouble himself at the time of his appointment for "speaking scandalous words against Charles Osborne, esquire," a Middlesex justice, "in the presence and hearing of divers of the ... King's lieges and subjects" on 18th December, 1685. It may well be that he accepted the post of hangman in an attempt to avoid punishment for the offence. If so, he did not succeed, for when he pleaded guilty to it at the Middlesex Sessions on 12th January, he was sentenced to pay a fine of £3.6s.8d, to be whipped at the cart's tail from Rosemary Lane to Hermitage Bridge and to "put in good sureties for his good behaviour during an entire year".

We do not know whether it was he who carried out two executions at Tyburn on 20th January, but it seems from a broadside *A Pleasant Discourse by way of Dialogue,   between the Old and New Jack Catch* (a copy of which is to be found in the Guildhall Library) that his own sentence of whipping was inflicted the following day. In this broadside, printed on 22nd January, Ketch mocks Rose over his 'race' from Rosemary Lane to the Hermitage, and goes on to give him the following advice:

Then henceforth learn for to be wise,
Or else't may worser be;
Consider in good manners lyes,
Your place o'th Tripple-tree:
The low Capers already you
Have most gentiely cut
Beware the high one ben't your due,
And I shall tye the knot.

This is of some interest to us in the light of what subsequently occurred.

Pascha Rose continued as hangman and received a free pardon on 26th February. Two months later he and another man, Edward Smith, were apprehended after breaking into the house of a William Barnet in the parish of Stepney and stealing "a Cambler Coat and other Apparrel, to the value of 20*s* and upwards."

They appeared for trial at the Old Bailey Sessions of 20th-22nd May, 1686, were convicted on 'very plain' evidence – part of the stolen property had been found in Rose's breeches – and sentenced to death.

"The 28th [May], five men of those lately con-demned at the sessions were executed at Tyburn; one of them was one Pascha Rose, the new hangman, so that now Ketch is restored to his place," recorded Luttrell.

*****

Ketch outlived Rose by only a few months; his own burial took place at St James's, Clerkenwell, on 29th November, 1686.

A letter from a Dr Hutton to Thomas Comber, the Dean of Durham, dated 4th December, states:

"Mr Johnson was whipped on Wednesday (1st December), but civilly used by the new hangman, Jack Ketch being buried two days before."

He had, it seems, continued working until the very end – and just as brutally as before. We may be sure his death was unlamented.

Hangmen with a Pedigree

Among Jack Ketch's Scottish contemporaries we find
one Alexander Cockburn, whose appointment as hangman of Edinburgh is recorded in the Town Council
Minutes of 1st July, 1681. He had previously been
hangman of Stirling, having there 'undermindit' his
predecessor, Mackenzie, "and got him thrust out of
his place". But why he left Stirling we do not know.

At any rate, he *did* leave, and it is known
that his first task as hangman of Edinburgh was the
burning of a quantity of contraband English clothes.
But he was not to remain in his new post for long,
for on 16th January the following year he was
brought to trial before the Provost and bailies of
Edinburgh, sitting 'as Sheriffs within themselves', for
the murder of John Adamson, a licensed beggar. Of
this case Sir John Lauder recorded that "[the]
probation was slender, and most of it by women...
and there was only presumptions against [the
prisoner]." - "as his denying that beggar was in his
house that day, the contrair whereof was proven;...
the finding [of] bloody cloaths in his house, [and] the
hearing [of] groans therfrae." But "the assize found
him guilty, and referred his wife Bessie Gall to the
Judges."

He was hanged and gibbeted on 20th January,
the sentence being carried out by Mackenzie, whom
he had 'undermindit' in Stirling. He died without

making a confession. Bessie Gall was banished.

The Edinburgh hangman at this time, as already explained, was called the *dempster* (or *doomster*) or, more commonly, the *lockman* while the hangman of Stirling was called the *staff man*. But the Edinburgh official sometimes had an assistant who, as it happens, was also called a *staff man*.

We have no reason to suppose that Mackenzie became the regular Edinburgh hangman. If he did, he was soon replaced, for the next hangman mentioned in the Town Council Minutes is Donald Monro (or Munro), whose dismissal from office, for 'many miscarriages' was recorded on 22nd August, 1684. It is possible, however, that he was Monro's assistant, in which case he would have been dismissed with him, for Lauder recorded, between 15th and 20th August:

"Monro, hangman of Edinburgh, and Mackeinzie his stafman, beats a poor beggar so, that he was in hazard of his life, wheron they ware deprived, and thrust into the theiff's hole... And one called Ormiston is created hangman."

If, as is generally assumed, most hangmen were of the lowest origins, John Ormiston was an exception, for *he* was a man with a pedigree. Descended from a respectable landowning family, he was apparently the only son of Robert Ormiston, who owned an estate in Dalkeith during the first two decades of the century.

No record of his birth has yet come to light. If it took place in Dalkeith, where his sister Helen was born in 1610, it must have been before the earliest known registers, which date from 1609. This would have made him at least 74 years old at the time of his appointment – which seems unlikely. So, in all likelihood, he was born elsewhere at a later date.

Robert Ormiston, who had been in trouble with the law for debt (among other things), parted with his estate in 1619. It is therefore possible that, in spite of his ancestry, John was not accustomed to wealth. It is known that he lived for over 20 years (1652-73) in Haddington and, for short periods, in Inveresk, Fogo, Westruther and Cranston before settling in Edinburgh; that he was married three times and left a widower twice, and that he had, in all, sixteen children, several of whom died young.

Whoever was responsible for the depletion of the family fortunes - or, rather, the fortunes of this particular branch of the family - John Ormiston must have been impoverished in his old age for, on arrival in Edinburgh in 1684, he accepted employment as a servant to Robert Mowbray, the keeper of the Correction House. It was after this that the post of hangman became vacant.

He was said, at the time of his appointment, to be "a well favoured, discreet fellow", but this could hardly have been the view of more illustrious members of the Ormiston family, for nobody who prided themselves on being respectable in those days would have admitted to having a hangman among their relatives. In spite of this, John remained in the post until his death four years later, perhaps assisted by his young son, George, who was one day to occupy it himself.

During the late seventeenth century Edinburgh's common place of execution was the Grassmarket. There, at the east end of the street, stood the Gallows Stone, a massive block of sandstone on which a gibbet was erected whenever an execution was due to take place. The site was regularly, though not invariably, used from the Restoration to the year 1784, the hangings being effected by turning the condemned off a ladder. As in England, hanging, even when followed by gibbeting, was not necessarily considered a harsh enough form of punishment in a particular case, so variations were employed.

On 24th February, 1688, Phillip Stanfield was "hanged, his tongue cutt out, and his hand cutt off" for murdering his father - and this proved to be an even more grotesque spectacle than intended, due to "[an] accident of the knots of the rope wherewith he was hanged, whereby his feet and knees were on the scaffold... which necessitate the hangman to strangle him."

So, while the Edinburgh functionary had far fewer executions to carry out than the hangman of London, his work was no less gruesome. In one respect it was more so, due to Scotland's quasi-official recognition of torture as a means of interrogation. It is known, for example, that William Carstares, who was to become one of William III's most influential advisers, was tortured in Edinburgh soon after Ormiston's appointment.

One imagines that a "well favoured, discreet fellow" would have less of a liking for this sort of work than men of rougher stock.

****

There is no mention in the Town Council Minutes either of thhe death of John Ormiston or the appointment of his son George, in his place, but in the *Register of Interments in the Greyfriars Burying-Ground* we find his burial recorded on 15th December, 1688. It is probable that George, though only about 16 years old at the time, succeeded him as executioner without formality.

He was, at any rate, the official hangman less than four years later, for it is recorded in *The Register of Marriages for the Parish of Edinburgh* that George Ormiston, *lockman*, was married to Jean Mason on 15th July, 1692. George's life was short and evidently unhappy. His first two children, both girls, died in infancy – Margaret in 1693 and Marion in 1695. His wife followed them to the grave on 14th June, 1696. His second wife, according to Thomas Lane Ormiston's *The Ormistons of Teviotdale* (1951) was Anna Coudon, who bore his third daughter, Jean, in 1697; but theirs seems not to have been a formal marriage, and on 18th September, 1698, he was married to Marion lightbodie. who bore him a further child, marie, in 1699. Jean and Marie also died young, though not in infancy.

Ormiston remained hangman during the last years of the seventeenth century when the calamitous state of the Scottish economy, after several bad harvests, must have made his right to levy market dues strongly resented by the city traders.

By the spring of 1700 the populace of Edinburgh was becoming desperate. A Scottish attempt at founding a colony at Darien on the isthmus of Panama - obstructed by William III - had failed through lack of resources. A second attempt had been about to fail for the same reason when a Spanish force, sent to attack the settlement, was itself routed on 15th February. The news of this victory, reaching Edinburgh in June, caused rejoicing in the streets and a general illumination of the houses. However, a mob soon gathered, attacking the homes of everyone who was suspected of not sharing their sympathies. Before long the city was in the hands of the rioters and some of the prisoners in the Tolbooth - including the author and printer of three seditious libels - were released.

When order had been restored a number of arrests were made and the author and printer gave themselves up to the authorities. Four men who had, it was claimed, been ring-leaders of the rabble, were committed for trial, but there were some weeks of delay and uncertainty before the verdicts of the court were announced. At last, *The Flying Post* of 6th-8th August reported:

Edinburgh. August 1. Yesternight the Criminal Court sat late upon the four Persons concerned in the late Mobb; and passed Sentence upon them as follows, Charles Weir, Cook to the Thistle-Tavern, is to be whipt at the Tolbooth Door, at the Cross and at the Trone [Tron], and then to stand in the Pillory on Wednesday next from 11 till 12 a Clock and to return to Prison till he find Sureties, that he shall never more be seen in this Nation after such a Day, he being seen in the Tolbooth with a Bagonet in his Hand.

"One *Achison* Servant to Captain *Douglas* and a Baker, are to stand upon the Pillory with him; and to return to Prison till they find Sureties that they shall never be seen within this City. The 4th one *Henderson* the Printer's Servant is only to stand on the Pillory, it being proved that he was sent to the Tolbooth by his Master, after he was relieved by the Rabble, to see for his Mistris."

In accordance with these sentences, the four men were taken out to the pillory and there exhibited on 7th August, but the crowd was enormous and very much on their side. The four were therefore cheered repeatedly and showered with flowers and an abundance of wine, sent to them by well-wishers, was consumed there and then, going about the pillory "like water". Afterwards the cook, Charles Weir, was "scourged most gently" by Ormiston.

The Edinburgh magistrates – that is, the Provost and bailies – were outraged by this snub to their authority. They ordered the hangman to be whipped for not doing his duty and had him put in prison while they sent for the Haddington hangman to carry out the sentence. This was in spite of Ormiston's claim that he had been threatened with death if he "laid on but one sore stroke". This sentence was not carried out, as the Haddington hang man, on arrival at Edinburgh, took fright at the crowds thronging the streets and fled.

"Thus, after waiting two hours in the windows, we are disappointed of the show, and the prisoner returned," wrote an observer. "The magistrates of Haddington (some say) find themselves concerned to present their hangman, and are to send to some neighbour-town for a day's work of theirs. In short, the common discourse is, that all this bustle is like to terminate, in fine, in a persecution of the hangmen hereabouts, and breaking some few officers (whereof I may be one) of the army."

Ormiston was not the only person to find himself in prison as a result of this affair, for in a report from Edinburgh dated 13th August and published in *The Flying Post* of 17th to 20th we discover:

"Seven or eight of the Servants of the Thistle-Tavern are imprison'd for bribing the Hangman that he should not whip the Cook their Fellow-Servant concern'd in the late Uproar..."

And the matter did not end there, either, for we learn from the following number of *The Flying Post* (20th-22nd August) that the magistrates were not alone in apportioning blame for what had occurred:

" Edinburgh, August 15. The Magistrates of this City have been reprimanded by the Privy Council, for not seeing the Sentence upon the 4 men concerned in the late Tumult, put in Execution, they having met with such Usage in their designed Punishment, as may rather encourage them to do the like in time to come, than deter them from it."

This new development did nothing to hasten Ormiston's return to favour and, although he escaped being whipped, he was not allowed to continue as hangman. The Town Council Minutes record that on 30th August John Stewart was appointed to take his place.

We do not know how long Ormiston remained in prison or how he made out after being released, but presumably he followed the progress of his successor with interest, for when Stewart himself gave offence he was there to offer his services afresh. Thus it came to be recorded that on 20th August, 1701, he was reinstated:

"The Councill being informed that ( ) Stewart present lockman had fled this Citie though he knew that one John Carss was to be executed. They therfore simpliciter depryve him of his office And ordaines the toun officers to search for him and

apprehend and secure him into the Thieves Hole And in like manner the Councill does repone George Ormistoun late lockman to his office... "

No doubt he returned to the post determined to avoid getting himself into any further trouble. He had, after all, been Edinburgh's public executioner for almost the whole of his adult life and had had, as far as we know, no experience of any other sort of work.

But this time he was not destined to keep the position for long, for the following year, at the age of 30 at most, he died. We do not know the cause or circumstances of his death and the exact date of it has not yet come to light. *The Ormistons of Teviot-dale* tells us only that it occurred in 1702, and the Town Council Minutes mention it only in connection with the appointment of his second successor, John Robertson, on 1st July that year.

Robert Chambers, in an article published in *Chambers's Edinburgh Journal* 22nd February, 1834, described him as "a reduced gentleman, the last of a respectable family who had possessed an estate in the neighbourhood of Melrose", and goes on to state that he had become hangman of Edinburgh after squandering his inheritance in his youth. The article continues:

"Notwithstanding his extreme degredation, this unhappy reprobate could not altogether forget his original station, and his former tastes and habits. He would occasionally resume the garb of a gentleman, and mingle in the parties of citizens who played at golf in the evenings on Bruntsfield Links.

"Being at length recognised, he was chased from the ground with shouts of execration and loathing, which affected him so much, that he retired to the solitude of the King's Park, and was next day found dead at the bottom of a precipice, over which he appeared to have thrown himself in his despair.

"This rock was afterwards called the Hangman's Craig "

The story, that Chambers later retold in at least two of his books, had evidently been put together from at least two different sources, one of which has regrettably not come to light during the researches carried out for the present account. It is inaccurate on several points, for Chambers did not know that both father and son were hangmen: he thought it was George who had been appointed after Monro's removal from office in 1684, not realising that he could only have been about 12 years old at that time.

It may well be that his death occurred in the manner described, for this would certainly explain why he died so young, but so far we have no evidence of it from contemporary accounts.

We do know, however, that his unenviable reputation survived him for, in a book about Melrose published 41 years later (which was clearly one of Chambers' sources), we find, at the end of a paragraph dealing with the possessions of the Ormiston family in that area, the following reference to him:

"It is said, that George Ormiston, late Hangman in Edinburgh was a Cadet of this Family, if not the Representative of it; a Memorandum to old Families not to be puff'd up with Pride on account of their Antiquity, for they know not what mean Offices they or theirs may be obliged to stoop to."

George's father, the man who had really been "obliged to stoop", had by this time been long forgotten. Apart from pieces of information drawn from official records, we know nothing whatever about him.

The Sailor, the Blacksmith
& the 'Bailiff's Follower'

The first eighteenth century hangman of London
whose name is known to us was Richard Pearse, who
in 1706 petitioned his employers, the Court of Aldermen, for subsistence. In his petition he stated that he
was a very poor man, fit for no other employment,
and prayed that he might be given something to
prevent him starving. The post must have become far
less remunerative than it had been under the Stuarts!
The Aldermen, however, did not regard him as a
deserving case and gave him nothing.

About 8 years later the post became occupied
by John Price, a tough, brutal, illiterate man, whose
name is already familiar to readers of *The Newgate Cal
endar* and Captain Alexander Smith *Lives of the High
waymen* Price did not become well-known during the
twelve months or so that he kept the post, but three
years afterwards, in conversations with the Rev Paul
Lorrain, Ordinary of Newgate (the prison chaplain),
he still called himself the 'finisher of the law'.
Clearly, it was an occupation for which he considered
himself well suited, and one imagines that if he had
remained in it for some years longer he might not
have ended his own life on the gallows.

There are only two accounts of Price's early
life. Of these, the one left by Captain Smith is
almost certainly fictitious and best ignored: the
other, written by the Ordinary, may be more

accurate, but there is no certainty of it.

At any rate, he is said, in the latter account, to have been born about 1677 in Old Soho, which was then in the Parish of St Martin-in-the-Fields. As a boy he was apprenticed to a rag merchant, his father, a soldier, having been killed in Tangier in 1684. After two years of serving as an apprentice he ran away and found employment loading rags onto wagons. Later he went to sea, serving aboard various men of war off and on for almost 18 years. It was after his discharge from the Navy that he became hangman of London.

The post, according to Bleackley, was at this time worth about £40 a year - a considerable income for a man of the lower classes - when fees, gratuities and other perquisites were taken into account; but Price drank heavily, "spending his money so fast, and beyond his comings in... thereby growing in Debt". This was to be the cause of his downfall.

One day in 1715 he was passing through Holborn, carrying the clothes of three culprits he had just hanged, when he was arrested for a debt of 7s.6d. He managed to avoid imprisonment by handing over to the bailiffs all the money in his pocket, together with the three suits, in settlement of the debt; but soon afterwards he was arrested for two further debts.

This time, having no means of repayment, he was thrown into the Marshalsea Prison, a William Marvell being appointed hangman in his place. As luck would have it, this occurred just as the post was about to become a lot more lucrative than usual, due to the executions following the 1715 rebellion.

Of Marvell's early life the only thing that is certain is that he was a blacksmith by trade. Captain Smith in *The Comical and Tragical History of the Lives and Adventures of the most Noted Bayliffs in and about London and Westminster* (1723) tells us

that he " had been condemn'd twice for his Life for
Theft" by 1706. It is known that a William Marvel,
alias Marven, an old offender, was sentenced to death
at the Old Bailey in 1709 for "privately stealing 20
Yards of Muslin, value 4 *l.*, the Goods of *Jeremy Shad
well* " of the Parish of St Magnus, and pardoned a
year later. Unforntunately, we cannot be sure that
Smith had any grounds for his claim that the old
offender convicted in 1709 was the same man. It
does, however, remain a distinct possibility, particularly in view of what was to happen to him later,
that Marvell *was* a convicted felon before his appoint
ment as hangman.

If so, it did not cause him to have any qualms
about his new work, for we learn from *The History of
the Press-Yard* (1717) that he received the news of
the surrender of the Jacobite army at Preston (13th
November, 1715) with joyful anticipation, celebrating
his good fortune in the company of "an Understrapper
to one of the Turnkeys... and a Deputy Bedmaker" in
Newgate Prison.

"Two or three hundred prisoners for high
treason!" he exclaimed. "Drink a bumper to their
sudden arrival! They'll be your tenants very speedily."

He was to receive, he said, a fee of £3 for
every peer he beheaded, as well as their clothes and
the money in their pockets - "and for every gentleman hanged and quartered I am to have the like sum,
with the respective gratifications they shall make me
for a quick and easy dispatch."

There were far fewer executions than he
expected, but he did well out of the rebellion all the
same. On 7th December he executed nine adherents
of the Pretender at Tyburn and on 24th February the
following year he beheaded the rebel lords Derwentwater and Kenmure on Tower Hill.

These and other executions resulting from the
rebellion caused the London hangman's income to rise
to more than double its usual level during the first
year that Marvell was in office - but they also made

him a notorious figure, a subject of rumours and an object of mockery.

On 9th March, 1716 - just a fortnight after the beheading of the rebel lords - *The Weekly-Journal or Saturday's-Post* reported that the hangman was "dangerously ill of a consumption." This is unlikely to have been true, for it appears that he executed 11 malefactors at Tyburn only three days later and no further reference to any such illness has been found among the newspapers of that year.

The following year *The Original Weekly Journal* of 24th-31st August reported in a less than reverent manner that he was dead:

"We hear that on Sunday last John Ketch, alias Marvell, Esq; Executioner-General of the County of Middlesex, Departed this Life at his House in Broad St Giles's, universally Regreted as well in regard of his Natural Experience and great Abilities in the due Performance of the several Parts of his Office, as for his agreeable Conversation..."

The obituary went on to claim that Marvell had been married twice; that he had had three sons by the first marriage, two of whom had been hanged and the third sentenced to transportation, and that he had been "Door-keeper to the Bear-Garden," - "which office he discharg'd with great Fidelity and Applause" - some years earlier. It said nothing of his having been a blacksmith. It concluded:

"The Corps of this great Person will be Interr'd some time next Week near Paddington, amongst those of his Ancestors. Who will succeed him in this Important Trust, is yet unknown; but there are already 14 candidates for it, among whom we hear are three Thief takers, two Disbanded Footmen, a broken Change broker, and two Prize-fighters."

There is no corroboration of any of the claims made in this 'obituary', and it is probable that there is little or no truth in any of them.

When later it was discovered that Marvell was not dead at all, the publisher of *The Original Weekly*

Journal saw no need to announce this fact.

After the unusually high earnings of his first year in office, the former blacksmith seems not to have been able to live on the lower income of the months which followed and, on 6th November, 1717, he was making his way to Tyburn to carry out three executions - we do not know why he had decided to go on ahead of the hanging-cart - when he, too, was arrested for debt.

He managed somehow to avoid being carried off to join John Price in the Marshalsea, but was then "set upon by the Mob, who beat and used him so unmercifully" that he was unable to hang the condemned. After a long delay at the Triple Tree, the exections had to be abandoned, the three prisoners being taken back to Newgate, "where it is said they must lie till *Jack Ketch* recovers of his Suffocation in the Horse-Pond, and is in Condition for his honest Employment".

As a result of this incident (which led to the three culprits having their sentences commuted), Marvell was unjustly removed from office, and almost prosecuted for "neglecting his duty", a man named Banks being appointed in his place. Banks was reported to be - of all things - "a Bailiff's Follower". The "Executioner-General" was not at all happy about being dismissed. It is even possible that he appealed for reinstatement, for *The Weekly-Journal or Saturday's-Post* of 30th November reported that "the Right Worshipful John Ketch Esq; [was] in a fair way of recovering his Post of Honour":

"It seems his Worship had petitioned the Sheriffs of London and Middlesex to be restored, and being resolved to speak handsomly to his Cause, dress'd himself up in the Trophies of his Office Vest, the fine Linnen, and embroider'd Wastcoat of two honest Gentlemen, that had pass'd under his Operation, over which he put a very handsom (BORROW'D) Coat, and so appeared in a Figure suitable to the Dignity of his Personal Employment."

But Marvell's efforts - if, indeed, there is any truth in the paragraph - were to no avail. He had done all the hanging that he was destined to do.

The same newspaper the following week reported the new hangman carrying out one of his tasks at the Old Bailey. Three soldiers had been brought to trial, but refused to plead to the charges against them. Banks had therefore to screw their thumbs together with whipcord - a recently-devised alternative to *peine forte et dure* (or pressing to death).*

John Price (according to the Ordinary) remained in the Marshalsea until early in 1718, when he and another prisoner got out through a hole in the wall and made good their escape; but it was not long before he was back in the hands of the law and this time he was in far more serious trouble. What had happened was that, on 13th March the same year, late at night, he had been walking drunkenly across Bunhill Fields when he ran into Elizabeth White, an old woman who sold cakes and gingerbread in the streets. He attacked her, intent upon both robbery and rape and, meeting resistance, beat her savagely. Two bypassers, coming to investigate the noise, found him "busy about her" - "with her Coats up to her Belly [and] Streams of Blood issuing out of her Eyes and Mouth". They seized him and, leaving his victim alone and unable to move, carried him off to a watch-house, where a constable detained him. When, later, the woman was attended to, she was found to have a badly bruised scalp, one eye knocked out of its socket, a bruised throat, a broken arm and a lacerated womb. She died of her injuries four days later.

Price was held overnight, then taken before a justice and committed to Newgate to await trial. When Elizabeth White died he was charged with murder.

*At this time a trial could not take place until the prisoner had pleaded to the charge or charges against him.

At his trial, which took place at the Old Bailey Sessions of 23rd-26th April, he pleaded not guilty. He claimed that, as he crossed Bunhill Fields on the night in question, he "found something lie in his way". He kicked at it and found it to be a woman, he said; he lifted her up, but found that she was unable to stand. It was while he was doing this that he was apprehended. The jury did not believe him. A newspaper reporting the case on 26th April said:

"[He] was found guilty, and is such a harden'd villain that he appeared not at all concerned, and went afterwards upon the Leads, and took the present Hangman by the Hand, telling he hang'd a great many, and now he must hang him."*

Back in Newgate, Price was secured in the condemned hold, with little chance of a commutation of sentence. In view of the enormity of his crime, he was to be hanged on a temporary gallows near the place where it had been committed; also, his body was to be gibbeted. There was, however, a delay of some weeks before the sentence was carried out.

"The Condemn'd Hold... lies between the Top and Bottom of the Arch under Newgate from whence there darts in some Glimmerings of Light, tho' very imperfect, by which you may know that you are in a dark, Opace, wild Room," says *The History of the Press-yard*.

"By the Help of a Candle... your Eyes will lead you to boarded Places, like those that are raised in Barracks, whereon you may repose your self if your Nose will suffer you to rest, from the Stench that diffuses its noisome Particles of bad Air from every Corner.

"If you look up, you see the Order of Nature inverted, by having the Commonside Cellar over you,

---

*The leads referred to here were more likely those at the front of the court-house, than those on the roof of the prison (as Bleackley assumed).

*or if you cast your Eyes downward, all Things are
equally surprising and unnatural.*

   *"Here lie Chains affix'd to Hooks, and there
Iron Staples are driven into the Ground to bring those
to a due Submission that are Stubborn and Unruly.*

   *"The Walls and the Floor are all of Stone, and
bear a Resemblance to the Hearts of those that
place you there..."*

The former hangman was allowed to drink spirits, and
did so to excess; a newspaper published on the day of
his execution said that "he hath since Sentence of
Condemnation been drunk for several Days suc-
cessively, and committed most horrid outrages".

   The Rev Paul Lorrain found that in drink he
was "Insensible of his Misery... and Unapprehensive of
his future state", and that, when sober, he "seem'd
to be a little more Considerate and Serious, and shed
some Tears either of Grief or Fear, or both, [and]
did then in the general lament his wicked Life... and
woful Condition", though continuing to deny that he
was guilty of the crime for which he had been
sentenced.

   Drinking was not his only diversion in the
condemned hold, as we discover from *The
Original Weekly Journal* of 7th-14th June:

   *"A Little Girl who used to carry Victuals to
John Price the Hangman in Newgate, has declared
that a few Days before his Execution, he had Carnal
Knowledge of her Body in the said [jail]."*

   No doubt this was one of the "most horrid
outrages" to which the other newspaper had referred.

   On 31st May, 1718, at the place of execution
in Bunhill Fields, Price finally confessed his guilt,
asked that the spectators should "take warning from
his untimely end", and begged their prayers. When
Banks had done his work, the body was taken to
Stonebridge, near Holloway, where it was hung in
chains later the same day.

   Two years later, on 28th May, 1720, *The Weekly·
-Journal or Saturday's-Post* reported:

"In the same Prison [Newgate] died one Price, Widow of the late Hangman, who, had she lived, was to have been transported."

William Marvell, after losing his position, had gone back to his former trade. He had a thin time, obtaining little work, and was sometimes forced to beg. He was, however, lucky enough to get an order for the suit of iron in which John Price was gibbeted.

On 7th August, 1719, he entered a haberdasher's shop in Coleman Street "with a Lock under his Arm and an Apron on" and began bargaining over the price of some silk handkerchiefs, carrying one of them to the door to show to a woman who was standing there. After he had left the shop ten other silk handkerchiefs were found to be missing from the counter. The shop-keeper's daughter ran out into the street to look for him, but by this time he was out of sight. He had been recognised by a woman standing at the door of a nearby alehouse, but six weeks elapsed before he was apprehended.

Confronted by the haberdasher's wife and daughter, Marvell admitted the offence, claiming that he had been drunk at the time. He offered to pay for the stolen handkerchiefs at a rate of a shilling a week, "he being poor", but the haberdasher insisted that he should be brought to trial. He was then taken before a justice and committed to Newgate, where, "being unruly, [he] was put into the Condemn'd Hold".

On 15th October he appeared at the Old Bailey, charged - as the *Old Bailey Sessions Papers* inform us - with "privately stealing 10 Silk Handkerchiefs, value 12s. out of the Shop of *Nathanael Simms*". He pleaded not guilty.

"The prisoner owned his being in the shop to buy a Handkerchief, but denied that he took any away, and said that he was prosecuted out of Malice, several having bore him ill Will for performing his Office in cutting off the Earl of Derwentwater's

Head", the *Sessions Papers* record.

*"He called several who gave him the Character
of an Honest and Industrious Man, and some of them
added, that they had heard him declare he resolved
to continue so as long as he lived, and that he would
rather beg than steal; for that if he should be taken
in Stealing but one penny, his very Character would
hang him..."*

He was on trial for his life (perhaps not for
the first time), for it was a capital offence to steal
from a shop to the value of five shillings, but the
jury, though convinced by the evidence against him,
were unwilling to send him to the gallows. They
therefore brought him in guilty only of stealing to
the value of 4s.10d.

The *Sessions Papers* tell us that he was there
upon sentenced to transportation – no specific term
is given – and that, on hearing this judgment "he
beg'd of the Court not to send him beyond [the] Sea;
but to admit him to any Corporal Punishment they
should think fit, which he would willingly submit to,
tho' it were to be Whipt a Mile". His plea went
unheeded.

On 23rd October, 1719, between 5 & 6 o'clock
in the morning, a party of convicts (about 80 by one
account, 91 by another) were taken from Newgate to
Blackfriars Stairs on their way to Woolwich, to be
put aboard a transportation vessel bound for America.

The Original Weekly Journal, noting Marvell's
presence in the group, was as facetious as ever,
stating that "tho' his Request was not fully answer'd,
as to his earnest Desire of being whip'd at home,
yet, in some Measure, it was granted, at his going
abroad, for they whip'd him away on board, among
the rest of his Brethren in Iniquity."

This is the last news we have about him. The
party of convicts was bound for Maryland; so perhaps
he completed his term and settled there, or perhaps
eventually returned to England; but we have no way
of knowing.

'Dick Arnold' and the Comical Fellow

Some time between 31st May, 1718, when John Price was hanged, and the early part of 1719, Banks was followed as hangman of London by Richard Arnet, who was often referred to by his contemporaries as 'Dick Arnold'.

Captain Alexander Smith tells us that on 13th February, 1719, when a number of executions were performed. the Ordinary of Newgate and *"Dick Arnold* the Hangman" both arrived at Tyburn with gloves and favours distributed by the thief-taker, Jonathan Wild, who was celebrating one of his marriages that day.

There is no corroboration of this in the surviving newspapers, although these did report the hangings. Not long afterwards there appeared a tract entitled *A Seasonable Hue and Cry after the Pretender* which purported to have been "formerly published [in 1716] by *John Price* my *Predecessor"* and was now "Faithfully and Historically continu'd... by me, *Richard Arnett,*Jack-Catch for the time being".

We may therefore be certain that Arnet was already hangman by the time Marvell fell foul of the law, and reasonably sure that he was in attendance at the Old Bailey (to inflict sentences of "burning in the hand" or deal with anyone who "stood mute") when the former occupant of his post pleaded to be whipped rather than transported.

He was to be the regular finisher of the law

for the next nine years, during which time he would execute many of Jonathan Wild's victims, including the jail-breaker Jack Sheppard and, later, Wild himself.

One of his early tasks, in all likelihood, was the whipping of a chairman named Moor from Somerset House to the Haymarket on 16th April, 1719, for insulting a member of the Royal Family. On that occasion, we are told, the hangman "follow'd his Work pretty close" and "made [the culprit] cry *God bless King GEORGE* before he had done with him". This pleased the spectators, many of whom "caress'd and applauded [him] after his Work was over".

The same enthusiasm was in evidence one day in 1725, when he hanged 8 malefactors, for a contemporary chronicler relates:

"The two Foot-Pads and Swaffo's Man, went to Tyburn in their Shrowds*; and the latter, when they were going to be ty'd up, slipp'd his Head out of the Halter, leap'd out of the Cart among the Mob, and began to tear off his Shrowd; but his Hands were ty'd, and he could do but little at it: Jack Ketch leap'd upon his Back, and the Sheriffs Officers surrounded him, so that he was soon taken, re-halter'd, and hang'd."

Arnet seems not to have been particularly unpopular. No doubt the alarming growth of crime in general in the south of England, reaching its climax during his tenure of office, made the hangman less objectionable to the populace than usual.

One of his clients in 1721 was William Spiggott, a highwayman, who refused to plead at the Old Bailey Sessions of 29th January. Arnet was ordered first to screw his thumbs with whipcord and then, when this proved unavailing, to subject him to the ordeal of *peine forte et dure* Spiggott endured weights totalling 350lbs on his chest for half an hour

---

*About this time it was becoming almost fashionable for criminals to be hanged in their burial shrouds.

but then, when another 50lbs was added, begged to be taken back to court to plead. He was hanged on 8th February.

Later the same year Nathaniel Hawes, another highwayman, was put to the same ordeal. He gave up after bearing weights of 250lbs for about 7 minutes, and was hanged on 22nd December.

Jack Sheppard was a robber and burglar renowned for his remarkable escapes from Newgate. When he was hanged on 16th November, 1724, the crowds fought over his body; one group had apparently made arrrangements for him to be resuscitated, while others feared that the body was being taken away for dissection and were determined to rescue it. The resulting riot was put down by a detachment of Foot Guards.

Jonathan Wild, whose thief-taking exploits included the capture of Spiggott and Hawes, as well as Sheppard, was also an organiser of criminal gangs; he had, in fact, gained control of most of London's underworld. He was finally sentenced to death for accepting money for the recovery of stolen property without having apprehended or trying to apprehend the thief concerned. When he rode in the cart to Tyburn in the company of two other prisoners, on 24th May, 1725, the mob were "so outrageous... in their Joy to behold him on the Road to the Gallows, who had been the Cause of sending so many thither, that they huzza'd him along to the Triple Tree, and shew'd a Temper very uncommon on such a melancholy Occasion, for they threw Stones at him; with some of which his Head was broke, and the two Malefactors, Sperry and Sandford, between whom he sate... were hurt."

At the place of execution he remained seated in the cart while the other two were waiting to be turned off, Arnet having told him that he could have "any reasonable Time to prepare himself", but soon the mob grew impatient. They "called out incessantly to the Hangman to do his Office, and threatened to knock him on the Head if he did not immediately perform it." Fearing for his own safety, Arnet gave way to their demand.

The following year Catherine Hayes was burnt at Tyburn for petty treason – the murder of her husband. It was customary by this time for the hang man to strangle women so sentenced before the flames reached them, and this Arnet tried to do by means of a rope passed through a hole in the stake, but as he did so the fire reached his hands forcing him to desist. The condemned woman was therefore burnt alive.

Spiggott, Hawes, Sheppard, Wild and Catherine Hayes were all celebrated criminals – Sheppard and Wild being among the most famous of all time; but of the man who officiated at their executions we know very little – less, in fact, than we know about either Price or Marvell – and nothing of his life before he became hangman.

He appears not to have been either a felon or a debtor and we have no reason to suppose that the Court of Aldermen was in any way displeased with the way in which he performed his duties. There are very few references to him by name in contemporary publications. It is known that he lived in Deptford and that he was buried at the church of St Nicholas beside the Green on the night of 13th August, 1728. It is known, too, that the chief mourners at his funeral were "Little Tom his truly lamenting Servant, and his Wife, &c.", but the only other thing we know about him is that he was paid a salary of £20 a year. For the executioner of Jack Sheppard and Jonathan Wild that really is very little!

His successor, John Hooper, is known to have been an assistant turnkey at Newgate Prison. In that or some other capacity in 1727 he had been given the duty of waiting on Major John Oneby, a privileged prisoner lying under sentence of death for killing another man in a coffee-house brawl. It is also

known that in May the following year he was escort-
ing Mary Jenkins, a capital offender, from the Old
Bailey back to Newgate Prison when an attempt was
made at a rescue. One source tells us that he was
'promoted' to the post of hangman "by Virtue of his
own personal Merit, [he being] without Bribery or
Corruption".

While such comments were generally made
ironically, in view of the disesteem in which executioners were held, it is possible that this particular
one was not, for the same source leads us to believe
that he was a likeable person with a talent for
jesting:

"[As] honest a Fellow as *Jack [Hooper] was,
yet, when the Keeper introduced him to the Major,
the Major it seems did not much like his Looks; for,*
says he, *What the Devil do ye bring this Fellow
here for? [Whenever] I look at him I shall think
of hanging.*

"A few Days, however, not only reconciled the
Major to his new Companion, but made him even fond
of his Company, for *Jack* was a comical Fellow: He
would tell a hundred wild, out-of-the-way Stories,
writhe his Face to all the Figures in Geometry,
preach Sermons, say his Prayers, and play a World of
Monkey Tricks, with which the Major was mightily
diverted..."

It is also possible that Hooper had a good
reputation in some quarters as a result of his conduct
during the attempted rescue of Mary Jenkins, when,
despite being struck on the head by "a lusty Fellow...
with a great Oaken Stick", he was able to prevent
his prisoner escaping.

Several newspapers mentioned the new finisher
of the law by name about the time of his appointment. *The Weekly Journal or British Gazetteer* of
17th August, 1728, and *The Gloucester Journal* of
three days later both referred to him as *Captain*
John Hooper, the latter describing him as "a Dealer

in Pack-thread"*. None of them mentioned his post at Newgate.

Brice's Weekly Journal of 30th August informs us that he was issued with "[a] Warrant from the Sheriffs... in the Words following, viz. 'These are to authorize and empower you John Hooper, to do Execution upon the Bodies of such Persons as shall be by Law appointed to suffer Death [at] Tyburn. Given under our Hands and Seals, &c.'" It appears that he had to produce this warrant before carrying out the execution of James Haddock, a thief, on 23rd August.

Hooper, like his predecessor, held office for some years. A receipt book kept by the Company of Barber-Surgeons reveals that he was given a Christmas box of 7s.6d. in each of the years 1729 to 1731 and that he was sufficiently literate to sign himself *John Hooper, Executioner* on two of the three occasions. In all likelihood he continued as hangman until late in 1734 or early in 1735.

Of the many executions carried out during this period, the most noteworthy was probably that of Sarah Malcolm, who was hanged on a gibbet in Fleet Street on 7th March, 1733, for the murder of her mistress, Mrs Duncombe, and two fellow servants. One account states that the prisoner "was dress'd in a black Gown, white Apron, Sarsenet Hood and black Gloves"; another that she "appeared very serious and devout, crying a wringing her Hands in an extraordinary Manner".

"She was assisted in her Devotions by the Rev. Mr. Peddington (of St Bartholomew the Great), and Mr. Guthrie (the Ordinary of Newgate) attended in the Cart. She declared to the People, that her Master knew nothing of her Intentions of the Robbery, &c. and said that she had given to Mr. Peddington a Letter, which related what she had to say to the Fact.

*The former stated that he was "a Person of known Probity and Integrity... who merits the Place by his unspotted Character".

"During the Time she was in the Cart, what with praying, Agony and Passion, she fell down; but immediately was rais'd, and laid her Head against Jack Ketch, and Mr. Peddington read to her: At length she was turn'd off, and hung about Half an Hour, and then cut down, and put in a Coach, and carried to the Pump-house at Newgate..."

A third account states:

"Several of the Nobility, and other Persons of Distinction, saw the Execution from the neighbouring Houses; and there was as great a Concourse of common People as ever was seen on the like Occasion. Many of the Spectators were hurt by the breaking down of a Scaffold; and very few of the Ladies and Gentlemen but had their Pockets either pick'd or cut off..."

A few weeks after this event a Mr Chevett or Chovet, a surgeon, tried to save the life of a condemned highwayman named William Gordon by inserting a silver tube in his windpipe before he was hanged, and bleeding and warming the body after it had been cut down. The attempt was unsuccessful.

Then, on 28th May the same year, we find:

" *John Jones* and *Jn Davis* condemn'd for Robberies on the Highway, were executed at *Tyburn*. *Davis* feign'd himself sick, and desir'd he might not be ty'd in the Cart: But when he came to the Tree, while the Hangman was fastening the other's Halter, he jumpt out of the Cart, and ran over 2 Fields; but being knock'd down by a Countryman, was convey'd back and hang'd without any more Ceremony."

It is tempting to assume, as Bleackley did, that Hooper used his talent for jesting to cheer the condemned as he rode with them in the cart to Tyburn, for this would certainly seem to have been in character with him, but no evidence of it has come to light.

In the newspapers of 1728-35 there are a number of reports of the use of the pillory, which was sometimes accompanied by a disturbance.

Criminals exhibited in this way were often treated savagely by the spectators, some of them dying as a result.

Hooper did not always officiate, though it was the hangman's duty to do so. He does not seem to have been present, for example, when John Waller was murdered while undergoing this form of punishment in 1732. He may not even have been there when Captain Thomas Hayes, a forger, stood in the pillory in 1729, in spite of the fact that his particular sentence included the cutting off of an ear.

He did, however, carry out the mutilation of Japhet Crooke (another forger) in 1731, for one account of this states:

"[The] Time being near expired, [Crooke] was set on a Chair on the Pillory, when the Hangman, dress'd like a Butcher, came to him, attended by two Surgeons, and with a Knife, made like a Gardiner's Pruning Knife, cut off both his Ears, and with a Pair of Scissers slit both his Nostrils, which were afterwards sear'd with a hot Iron; all which he bore most surprizingly, till his Nostrils were burnt, which put him to great Torture..."

Like his predecessors, Hooper had many whippings to inflict in public; it seems, too, .that he was also expected to carry out 'private' whippings at Newgate. One such whiping was reported in *The British Journal* of 21st February, 1730.

We also find that soon after the execution of Sarah Malcolm he had a libellous publication to burn:

"Monday Night last about Nine o'Clock the Daily Courant was publickly burnt by the Hands of John Hooper, the common Hangman, at Temple-Bar, for containing false and scandalous Reflections on the Merchants and Traders of this City, for their Opposition to the Excise."

We do not know whether Hooper died in office or ceased to be hangman for some other reason; a search of many of the newspapers of the period has failed to throw any light on the question. The earliest indication that he had departed is to be found in *The Old Whig* of 13th March, 1735, which informs us that a new hangman had officiated at Tyburn three days earlier.

Richard Arnett at an execution at Tyburn in 1724

The Impulsive Hangman

John Thrift was illiterate, nervous and hotheaded. His appointment as hangman of London is unrecorded, but he is believed to have been the new man who carried out 13 hangings on 10th March, 1735. There are, however, no references to him by name in any of the London newspapers until 25th May the following year, when this paragraph appeared in *The General Evening Post:*

"*Yesterday about Nine in the Evening was committed to Newgate by Justice Midford, John Thrift, otherwise call'd Jack Catch on the Oath of Mary White, for assaulting and knocking down, and forcibly taking away from her, in his own House, a strip'd Ticken Pocket, in which were 3s.6d. He was but just return'd from doing his Duty at Tyburn when he committed the above Robbery.*"

We know nothing of Thrift's personal circumstances at this time; we do not know whether he was even acquainted with Mary White. We may be sure, though, that he protested his innocence with vigour.

Less than two weeks later it was reported that "the Imprisonment of John Thrift... being on a malicious Prosecution... he has been bailed by order of the Sheriffs and accordingly set at Liberty; and [Mary White] is committed to Newgate in his stead, to be tried at the next Sessions at the Old Bailey".

It is clear from these two paragraphs that

Thrift was not new to his post at the time. The assumption that he had been appointed the previous year is therefore a reasonable one. It is even possible that Mary White was a relative or close friend of somebody he had hanged. We have no means of ascertaining this, however, as the case against her was never taken to court.

Thrift, at any rate, acceded to the office *about* 1735 and he remained in it until his death in 1752. During that period the gallows was the scene of many outrages, some of them resulting from the growing public abhorrence of the anatomists, who required the bodies of hanged felons as subjects for dissection.

On the day that Thrift was committed to Newgate, for example, the mob at Tyburn fought "a terrible Battle" with constables of the Holborn Division in an unsuccessful attempt to prevent the body of George Ward, who had been hanged for robbing and shooting at a baker in Islington, being taken away for this purpose.

Anatomisation was only one reason, for two months later Thomas Reynolds, a turnpike-leveller, was found to be still alive after being cut down from the Triple Tree and, when Thrift tried to hang him again, "the Mob... cry'd Save his Life, and fell upon the poor Executioner... and beat him in a most miserable Manner". Reynolds was carried off to a house in Acton and put to bed, but later died after being given a glass of wine.

In 1738 a party of sailors rescued one of their fellows from the hangman's clutches at Execution Dock in Wapping, where those malefactors whose offences had been committed at sea were hanged on the foreshore; in 1740 another culprit was found to be still alive after being hanged at Tyburn and in 1743 *The London Evening-Post* of 18th-20th January recorded:

"*Yesterday Morning, between Nine and Ten o' Clock, Thomas Rounce, condemn'd for High Treason,* in fighting against his King and Country on board a Spanish Privateer, was carried from Newgate on a Hurdle, drawn by four Horses, adorn'd with Ribands, to Execution-Dock. One of the Sheriffs Officers carried a Silver Oar before him.

"Jack Ketch rode upon the Hurdle, dress'd in a White Frock, with a Knife and Steel by his Side, and a drawn Scymetar in his Hand.

"After he had hung about 15 Minutes, the Executioner cut him down, ript up his Belly, and threw his Heart and Bowels into a Fire prepar'd for that Purpose. He was then quarter'd, and his Quarters put into a Coffin, and deliver'd to his Friends.

"The Crowd was so great that several People had their Legs and Arms broke, and were otherwise terribly bruised."

The disturbances and mishaps occurred regularly throughout the period that Thrift was finisher of the law. Yet, surprisingly, he seems to have left the place of execution unscathed on almost every occasion.

There were times when his nervous and impulsive nature must have brought his suitability for the post into question.

In January, 1741, we find that he was "committed by Justice Hervey to the Gatehouse for an Assault" - a committal which, like the earlier one, appears to have come to nothing. We find also, in the *Annals of the Barber-Surgeons:*

"24th September, 1741. John Thrift the Executioner this day attended on a complaint made against him by the Beadles for obstructing the Bodys being brought from Tyburne to the Hall for dissection and threatning to prevent the Company's measures for obtaining the same, when after he had been reproved, was Dismissed, But the Court [the Court of Assistants of the Company of Barber-Surgeons] then agreed (in order to prevent his intended proceedings) to attend the Lord Mayor and Court of Aldermen that they may on complaint be releived therein."

In spite of his shortcomings, he was regarded by General Williamson, the Lieutenant of the Tower, as "a good sort of man" - or so Williamson told Lord Kilmarnock on the eve of the latter's execution. But when Kilmarnock appeared on the black-draped scaffold on Tower Hill on 18th August, 1746, the hangman's nerve failed him: he burst into tears and had to be fortified with wine before he could perform his duty. Nonetheless, he did, going on to behead a second rebel lord, Balmerino, on the same scaffold almost immediately afterwards.

It is also worthy of note that three years earlier Thrift had personally apprehended a boy of 12 who had stolen three large silver spoons, three tea-spoons and a salt-spoon, and given evidence against him at the Old Bailey. The boy, Evan Evans, had been sentenced to seven years' transportation.

Whatever difficulties he had had with the law during the years 1736 and 1741, they were trivial in comparison with that which awaited him in 1750 - in the light of which he appears not to have been such a "good sort of man" at all.

On 11th March that year he was involved in an affray near his home in Coal Yard, Drury Lane (an alley running parallel with High Holborn),* in the course of which a David Faris was struck several times with a hanger and fatally wounded.

The weapon was Thrift's own and it was alleged that he had been the person who struck the blows. He was, in consequence, committed to Newgate and later indicted for murder.

The incident had started when Faris, his wife (who had a child in her arms) and two companions, Timothy Garvey and Patrick Farrel, passed by Thrift's house and the hangman's wife - who seems to have

* It was also in Coal Yard that Thrift had apprehended Evan Evans.

been a quarrelsome woman – overheard one of them
(Farrel) saying something about Jack Ketch. The
remark incensed her and she rounded on them insult-
ingly. A moment later Thrift came on to the scene
(if he was not there already) and struck Farrel two
or three times in the face.

Garvey managed to restrain him, suggesting, by
way of an excuse, that Farrel was "a little in
liquor". Thrift then went indoors and the four companions went on their way.

Thrift was not finished with them yet; taking
off his hat, coat and wig, he left the house brandish-
ing the hanger. The three men fled, leaving Rebecca
Faris and the child behind, but the hangman pursued
and soon caught up with them. It was then that Faris
was attacked and wounded, while his companions, it
seems, were engaged in fighting with one or two of
Thrift's associates. The affray must have continued
for some time, for it was said to have been watched
by a crowd of about a thousand people.

Covered in blood, Faris was carried to the
house of the magistrate, Henry Fielding, before whom
both he and his wife swore that the wounds had been
inflicted by Thrift. He was then taken to hospital.
The following day Thrift went to see Fielding himself
and asked for a warrant to be issued for a violent
assault, presumably against Faris. The magistrate
refused the application, saying that he had already
issued a warrant in connection with the incident and
could not grant cross-warrants. He advised the hangman to find somebody to stand bail for him.

A day or two later Thrift was brought back
before Fielding after surrendering himself to a constable, but was then refused bail and committed to
prison after a surgeon, Robert Heathfield, had told
the magistrate that Faris was unlikely to recover.

Faris died on 19th March and, on 27th April,
Thrift was brought to trial at the Old Bailey, charged
with his murder: he pleaded not guilty.

Rebecca Faris, Timothy Garvey and Patrick

Farrel all appeared against him, each giving an account of what had taken place and claiming that Thrift had struck the blows which caused the death of David Faris. This was corroborated by the next three witnesses.

Robert Heathfield then gave evidence about the victim's condition on arrival at hospital. "There was a piece cut out of the left side of his head, through the first table, flesh and all," he declared. "There were four other wounds on different parts of his head, and a wound on his left wrist. I imagined they were from some cutting instrument." He also told the court of two occasions on which the patient had informed him that Thrift had been his assailant.

"I did not give the blow," said the prisoner. "Enoch Stock" (an acquaintance of his) "did take the hanger out of my hand, and cut this man, the deceased."

Seven more witnesses then appeared, each claiming to have seen Thrift striking the blows, but the hangman stuck to his story, as the *Sessions Papers* show:

" *Prisoner.* I had been twice at St Giles's church that day, and as I was coming home through Drury-lane, Farrel began the quarrel. There were four of them, the deceased's wife was one, with a child in her arms. I turned into the Coal-yard where I live. "Blood and ounds, said Farrel, do you know who this is coming along? No, said the deceased, I do not know him; he said again, that is Jack Ketch, he stole a gold watch, and two silver spoons, and has broke out of Newgate.

"Said I, go along, you black-guard dog; they said, there was ten guineas reward for taking of me. Farrel knock'd me down at my own door. I strove to take the stick out of his hand, the others of them gave me another blow, and knock'd me down again.

"I desired my wife to fetch the hanger, and I do declare it never was out of the scabbard, till Enoch Stock took it out."

A man named Elliot, who seems to have been involved in the fighting, appeared on Thrift's behalf. Enoch Stock had snatched the weapon from the prisoner's hand, he said, "and fought his way through the mob to Short's-gardens," where the wounding took place. Afterwards he (the deponent) "took the hanger from Enoch Stock, and brought it to the prisoner's house".

Elliot concluded his evidence by stating: "I live in the prisoner's house. Since he has been in trouble I have done business for him." (In other words, he had substituted for Thrift at the gallows.)

There then followed three more witnesses for the prisoner, the first two saying they had seen Enoch Stock using the hanger, and the third that he had seen no hanger at all, but had heard somebody in the crowd at Short's Gardens swear that he would "cut Jack Ketch's brains out".

At this point Thrift asked for Stock to be called as a witness. "He knows, and has owned he did it, and I think he will not deny it," he said.

Stock had indeed declared, before Justice Fielding, that he had struck the blows against David Faris. As a result, he, too, had been committed to prison, although no proceedings appear to have been started against him. But now, though he gave evidence for the defence, his deposition fell short of the hangman's expectations:

" *Enoch Stock.   On the 11th of March, I was drinking a pint of beer at a publick house in Drury-lane with a friend. About a quarter of an hour after five in the evening, I parted with him, and was standing to make water; I heard a great noise, and I went up to the mob to see what was the matter, as far as the gateway near Short's-gardens. I heard the prisoner say, you thieves, have you a mind to murder me: they were beating him with sticks, four of them. He said, for God's sake, help me, for these rogues will kill me.*

"When he saw me, I had known him nineteen

or twenty years. I did not see him hit any of them, but stood against the wall in a white flannel waist-coat. They knock'd me down several times, and broke my head in several places, also my little finger in defending my head. I was quite stunned and lost my senses; I strove to get up two or three times, and they knocked me down again. I went home hanging on the prisoner's shoulder.

"He produced his shirt all bloody, &c.

"Q.Did you see the hanger?

"*Stock*.Yes, but I do not know what became of it. I do not know how I got [away], they beat me so unmercifully."

In spite of his denials and the evidence of the defence witnesses. Thrift was convicted of the murder and sentenced to death. To the delight of the regular Tyburn mob, he returned to Newgate with the dismal prospect of being hanged upon his own gallows.

Having been convicted of such a grave crime, Thrift could have had little hope of mercy - but mercy was to be afforded him nonetheless.

On 10th May he was respited for fourteen days, and when that period expired he was further respited "during the Pleasure of the Lords of the Regency".

It was then announced that he had been ordered for transportation for fourteen years.

Yet he was not destined for the plantations of North America either!

On 4th August the newspaper *Old England* stated:

"It is said that Thrift, the Executioner, will plead his Majesty's most gracious Pardon at the next Sessions at the Old Bailey."

And on 22nd September:

"A Free Pardon came for John Thrift the Hang-man, last Saturday... and he is to resume his Profession the next Execution."

In fact, he was back at work sooner than that, for on 24th September "a Woman was whipped at the

Cart's Tail, thro' Piccadilly, (by John Thrift lately pardoned) pursuant to her Sentence, at the last Sessions at the Old Bailey". Three days later a man was similarly whipped along Parliament Street for stealing saws.

The next executions were those of the highway-man, James Maclean, the forger, William Smith and ten others who were hanged at Tyburn on 3rd October.

To the populace of London it must have seemed extraordinary that Thrift, a convicted murderer, should have been back in his post after an absence of little more than six months, when so many others were hanged for lesser crimes. And we may be sure that he was more hated now than he had been at any time during his tenure of office.

The Court of Aldermen had reservations about retaining his services and it was reported only two weeks after the hanging of Maclean and Smith:

"The Sheriffs of this City have appointed a Person to succeed John Thrift, as Executioner for London and Middlesex."

Yet somehow he managed to hold on to the office until his death on 5th May, 1752, when he was succeeded by Thomas Turlis.

Six days after his death, Thrift's body was taken to St Paul's, Covent Garden, for burial. This caused much annoyance to the local people, for the burial ground had been "so much raised of late Years, that it [advanced] near to the Parlour Windows of the adjoining Houses", and the hangman, not having been resident in the Parish, was regarded as having no right to interment there.

The funeral was watched by a large, hostile crowd and the attendants (among whom was the newly-appointed Turlis) had to carry the coffin into the church to avoid trouble.

Later, when the danger had subsided, it was taken back outside and buried without incident.

The Last Hangman of Tyburn

At the time of his appointment as hangman of London Thomas Turlis was said in one newspaper to have been John Thrift's deputy for "many years". This could not have been entirely true, as only two years earlier the man Elliot had "done business" at Tyburn while Thrift was awaiting trial. He may, however, have been an occasional assistant to Thrift for some years and it seems likely that he had begun to deputise for him during his last year or two. This, at any rate, would account for the swiftness of his appointment as well as his attendance at the former hangman's funeral.

He was to be hangman in his own right. for almost nineteen years.

He began with a deputy of his own, but did not keep him for long, for *Read's Weekly Journal or British Gazetteer* of 23rd May, 1752, records:

"Tuesday a Man was committed to Newgate by Sir George Champion for stealing a Cask of Snuff. He was Deputy to Thomas Tullis (sic), who a few Days since succeeded the late John Thrift as publick Executioner."

The *Old Bailey Sessions Papers* of 25th–30th June reveal that the fellow in question was Joseph Barnet; that the cask itself was valued at 4d and the snuff inside it at £7 and that the offence had been committed on 16th April.

When the value of the goods was 40s or over in this type of theft the crime was a capital one, but, as in the case of Marvell, the jury chose to devalue the goods rather than send the prisoner to the gallows; they valued the cask and snuff together at 39s.: Barnet was accordingly sentenced to seven years' transportation.

Turlis, whose name was often given as Tullis or Tollis in the newspapers, was evidently a literate man; a reproduction of one of his bills in *The Hangmen of England* shows that he wrote in a fine copper-plate hand.

It seems, too, that he was well thought of by the sheriffs, for, in January, 1763, when he was caught stealing coal from a neighbour - the only occasion on which he ever broke the law, as far as we know - they prevented his prosecution and even obtained an additional post for him (that of hangman of Surrey) to increase his income.

Among the early executions taking place during Turlis' long career was that of Thomas Wilford, a one-armed youth of 17, who was hanged on 22nd June, 1752, for murdering his wife in a fit of jealousy; he was the first to suffer under a new Act of Parliament under which the bodies of all executed murderers were to be either dissected or gibbeted. We also find that of Dr Archibald Cameron, a physician, who was executed for high treason on 7th June the following year.

In 1759 the use of the Triple Tree was brought to an end. A new movable gallows was used in its place, being erected at a nearby site whenever an execution was to take place. For the execution of Earl Ferrers, who was hanged on 5th May, 1760, for killing his servant, a drop was used, part of the floor of the scaffold being raised about eighteen inches, with a contrivance for lowering it when the condemned was ready to be turned off, but this did not come into general use.

Hangings continued to be carried out from the

back of a cart until 1783, when Tyburn ceased to be a place of execution.

Ferrers arrived at the gallows in his own landau, drawn by six horses. He was to be hanged with a silken rope which he had provided himself and, as always when a nobleman was to be executed, the hangman had to beg his forgiveness before going about his work. Ferrers had a gratuity for him, but gave it to his assistant by mistake, with the result that "an unseasonal dispute ensued between those unthinking and unfeeling wretches".

Of the many culprits hanged on the movable gallows while Turlis was in office the most notorious was undoubtedly Elizabeth Brownrigg, who had flogged her female servant to death. She was executed on 14th September, 1767, her body being afterwards dissected at Surgeons' Hall.

The most pathetic was probably Cornelius Saunders, a poor-sighted man, who had stolen the savings of a fish-woman in Spitalfields. During the riot following his execution on 24th August, 1763, the home of his prosecutrix was ransacked and her furniture burnt.

Turlis officiated at Tyburn for the last time on 27th March, 1771. Five were hanged on that occasion, four of whom were reported to have "behaved in the press yard in a most audacious manner, and struck the Executioner when put into the Cart".

Early in April he died "on the road" after attending the assizes at Kingston.

There is no record of the appointment of his successor. The next hangman of London of whom we know anything was Edward Dennis, who may (or may not) have been appointed at Turlis' death and was almost certainly in office by 1774-5, when a William Brunskill was engaged as assistant hangman. Dennis and Brunskill were to carry out hangings both at Tyburn and at Newgate Prison.

Dennis' victims included the twin brothers,

Robert and Daniel Perreau (hanged for forgery in 1776), Dr William Dodd (also for forgery, in 1777), and the Rev James Hackman (for murder in 1779). It was also during Dennis' tenure of office that many people were hanged for taking part in the Gordon Riots, which took place in June, 1780, Dennis himself being involved in them. *The St James's Chronicle* of 13th-15th of that month announced:

> *"On Monday Night the Person commonly called Jack Ketch was apprehended at the Sign of the Blue Posts, an Alehouse in Southampton-Buildings, Holborn, on Suspicion of being a Ring-Leader in the late Riots. He was carried to Lincoln's Inn, and after Examination committed."*

On 3rd July he appeared for trial at the Old Bailey, charged with a capital offence.

The indictment against him charged "that he together with twenty other persons, and more, did, unlawfully, riotously, and tumultuously assemble on the 7th of June, to the disturbance of the publick peace, and did begin to demolish and pull down the dwelling-house of Edmund Boggis," a chandler, in New Turnstile, Holborn. He pleaded not guilty.

The rioting had actually started some days, before, in opposition to the recent Catholic Relief Act; the sacking and burning of homes, both of Catholics and of advocates of religious tolerance, had taken place in several parts of London, and it was to be a few more days before order was fully restored.

On the day in question, Mr Boggis had found a mob gathering outside his home between six and seven o'clock in the evening; fearing for his safety, he fled from the house. The mob forced an entry and began to remove his furniture, carrying it out to a nearby fire with cries of joy. Later, when he returned, Mr Boggis found that the place "was torn almost all to pieces".

Dennis lived in nearby Newtoners Street and each of the other four prosecution witnesses said that they knew him. According to one of them, he had been "the most active person amongst the whole mob". A second witness stated: "On the 7th of June I was opposite New Turnstile, near the Vine Tavern, which is about thirty or forty yards from Mr Boggis's. It was between the hours of six and seven. I saw the prisoner come down the Stile with a large piece of wainscoting. He put it upon the fire and gave a great huzza." He had seen the hangman returning two or three times for the same purpose.

Mr Boggis had not seen the prisoner among the mob; his evidence merely established that the house had been destroyed. It appears, however, that he had seen Dennis assisting in the demolition of another building the previous day.

The hangman admitted having taken part in the riot, but pleaded that he had been forced to do so. He said that he had been out to borrow money from a friend, having been unable to raise any on his salary, and had run into the mob on his way home.

"They made me carry wood several times, and I huzza'd by their orders several times," he said. "They swore they would use me ill if I did not." He added: "I kept myself from all other riots; I never was found out at a late hour. I was always abed before candle-light during the riots, because I would keep from the mob. I was vastly afraid of them; I knew they would use me ill."

He also claimed: "I have served the sheriffs a good while and they never heard any bad character of me."

Two of the witnesses were recalled and asked whether they had observed any threat of violence on the part of the mob towards the prisoner. They both replied in the negative.

Another was recalled to verify that he had seen the prisoner arrive with the mob. He did so.

After considering the case for only ten minutes, the jury brought the hangman in guilty. He was accordingly sentenced to death.

But he was not to be hanged (except in *Bar—*

naby Rudge), for soon afterwards the sentence was respited "during his Majesty's pleasure". He afterwards obtained a free pardon.

He had not been confined in Newgate, for this building – the reconstruction of which had been completed only three years earlier – had largely been destroyed during the rioting. We thus find, in *The Gentleman's Magazine*:

"The humanity of Mr Smith, the keeper of Tothillfields bridewell, to whose custody he was committed, deserves due praise. He declined confining him among the other prisoners lest his obnoxious character should expose him to their rage."

Whether he hanged any of his fellow rioters we do not know. The first batch, on 11th July, were hanged by "Deputy Jack Ketch", i.e., Brunskill. It is possible, though, that Dennis was released in time to hang some of the others.

In all, 29 people were hanged between 11th July and 9th August, all but four of them for rioting. The rioters were all hanged near the places where their offences had been committed, the others at Tyburn.

An observer noted "that all those Persons who have suffered Death for being concerned in the late dreadful Riots, are all hanged with a double Cord, twisted round their Necks, whereas those executed at Tyburn are always hanged with a single one."

The conduct of the hangman (or deputy hangman) during this period was both brusque and careless; the condemned suffered unnecessarily, the spectators were offended, and the culprit was criticised for appearing "to have as little *Feeling* as the Rope or Gallows by which he earns his Bread".

"A Correspondent says, that however great an Ignominy the Force of Prejudice may have stamped on the Office of Public Executioner, the present Jack Ketch is a Disgrace even to that Ignominy; for he handles the unhappy Convicts with as little Concern as a Butcher would a Sheep or Bullock," said *The Pub-*

lic Advertiser of 11th August.

"And tho' it were impossible to humanize this Savage, or tincture, by the strongest Exhortation, his debased Soul with Benevolence, yet he might at least learn to be decent. On Wednesday last he threw off the Hat of one of the unfortunate Sufferers, in a Manner that merited the severest Censure; and for other brutal Acts, he was much [booed] by the Populace."

In spite of all this criticism, the 'savage' remained in office, either as hangman or as assistant hangman, for Dennis and Brunskill continued working together for the next six years.

During the course of those six years, Francis Henry de la Motte was drawn, hanged and quartered for high treason (in 1781), William Wynne Ryland was hanged for forgery (1783) and Phoebe Harris was burnt for coining (1786). There were many multiple executions, the number of prisoners being hanged together being ten or more on several occasions, and twenty on one of them in 1785.

The hangman's income in 1780 included a salary of £30 a year, with fees of 6s.8d for each hanging and 5s for each whipping; he had, however, to pay for the services of his assistant out of his own pocket.

His perquisites could still be of considerable value to him, as we discover from an account of the execution of de la Motte:

"About nine o'clock the wretched culprit experienced the first instance of the succeeding miseries which he had to encounter, in the degrading circumstance of tying the arms behind with the very halter that was afterwards to hang him.

"On this occasion, M. De la Motte mistaking one of the Officers employed in this duty for the Executioner, gave him five guineas. This produced a warm dispute; the Executioner insisting on his right. Mr Akerman (the jailer of Newgate) was applied to by M. De la Motte to adjust this matter, and he *ordered the money to the Executioner."*

At Tyburn, after the prisoner had been hanging for half an hour – for it was customary by now for such prisoners to be left to hang until they were dead – "a venerable looking Gentleman... purchased his stock, handkerchief, and hat, at the price of some gold" rather than allow them to fall into the hangman's "unhallowed hands". This gold must also have gone to Dennis, as each of the items purchased was his by right.

It was not often that Dennis did as well as this out of individual executions, for there were few convictions for treason at this time, and wealthy clients had become few and far between.

On the other hand, clothes, even of ordinary criminals, were generally worth something to him, and the frequency of multiple executions ensured a regular supply of them. *The Attic Miscellany* (1791) states that an eccentric fortune-teller known as 'Old Cain' had a robe which he had "purchased of E Dennis, Esq. alias Jack Ketch! being that given him by the sheriffs in 1785, but laid by on account of its inconvenience", but we do not know whether there is any truth in this.

When Tyburn ceased to be a place of execution the condemned of London and Middlesex were hanged on a scaffold outside the Debtors' Door at Newgate – the prison having been rebuilt once again. A drop was used now, but the prisoners were still executed in batches. The crowds were as large and disorderly as ever.

"The whole erection is hung in black," wrote an observer in *The Gentleman's Magazine* in 1783.

"The criminals are attended, by the proper officers and the Ordinary of Newgate, from their cells to that part of the scaffold... which is a platform raised about two or three inches above the general floor... and directly under the gallows: here, after the usual prayers and solemnities, the rope is tied up, and, at the Sheriff's signal, the executioner

pulls away a staple... which loosens a bar that supports the platform... and the platform then falls in: and this being much more sudden and regular than that of a cart being drawn away, has the effect of immediate death.

"During the whole time of this awful spectacle, a full-toned bell, which is suspended above the roof of this part of the prison, is solemnly tolled...

"The scaffold is supported by strong posts, fixed into grooves made in the street and the whole is temporary, being all calculated to take to pieces, which are preserved in the prison."

Contrary to the belief of this observer, the scaffold was to prove to be primitive, a drop of only a few inches being far from sufficient to ensure immediate death. At this stage, in fact, it was hardly an improvement on the horse and cart: the hangman would often have to swing on the bodies to hasten the process.

Edward Dennis died in office on 21st November, 1786, his death being reported in *The Daily Universal Register* (afterwards *The Times*) the following day:

"Yesterday died at his apartments in the Old Bailey, as *regretted* in death as he was *respected* through life - Mr Dennis - commonly called *Jack Ketch*.

"In his office of *Finisher of the Law, Surveyor of the New-drop,* and *Apparitor of the Necklace,* alias *Yeoman of the Halter,* &c. he acquitted himself with the approbation of all - but the parties concerned.

"He had frequently a numerous company at his *levee,* tho' all complained of a want of variety in his dish, which was *hearty-choak* and *caper sauce.*

"He has on his death bed recommended his son to the *succession,* declaring him fit for that or any other office in which his Majesty may be pleased to employ him."

He was buried at St Giles-in-the-Fields on

26th November.

    The day after Dennis' death Brunskill hanged
seven people at Newgate. Having done so, he "turned
round to the populace, and making a   *profound bow*
seemed to enquire how they approved his*first perfor-*
mance. " He was to be hangman of London for the
next 28 years.

A Smithfield execution carried out by Thomas Turlis in 1761.

A Dumfries Hangman

Roger Wilson was appointed hangman of Dumfries on 17th April, 1758, with a salary of £6 a year and an allowance of £1.13s.4d for his house-rent. He remained in this post for the next 27 years, carrying out "not only the sentences pronounced by the magistrates of the Burgh, and of the King's judges on their circuits, but also the sentences of the sheriff, and of the justices of the peace at their quarter-sessions". He was also the town cryer - a separate post to which he had been appointed on 3rd December, 1760.

It was said of him that he was "a respectable man, if such a term can be applied to a hangman; kept cows, sold milk, and had two daughters, who, for beauty and good behaviour, were the admiration of all the youth of the place".

He had, in addition to his salary and free house, the right to a ladleful of meal, peas, beans or potatoes from every sack brought by traders into the market-place. It was thus customary for him to appear there every Wednesday, followed by a girl (perhaps one of his daughters) carrying a number of bags, into one of which he would empty his ladle each time it was filled.

Being discreet and modest, and in the practice of taking only half a ladleful out of the smaller sacks, he was on good terms with the dealers for many years, but the custom was resented and one day in 1781 a John Johnstone, of the Parish of Tinwall, "not only refused the hangman his dues, but abused and threatened him into the bargain".

Roger Wilson complained to the magistrates about this denial of his rights and Johnstone, refusing to discuss any possibility of a compromise, was sent to jail. However, "he was soon liberated, as he threatened to prosecute the magistrates for wrongous imprisonment".

It was soon clear that he was not acting just on his own account, but with the backing of others. The town council therefore asked the advice of Andrew Crosbie, a distinguished advocate, on the matter.

A memorial drawn up on the council's behalf set out the hangman's terms of employment. This admitted that it was not known "how the custom came to be introduced, [or] whether there ever was any agreement thereanent betwixt the town and County," but asserted "that such custom or tax has been levied past the memory of the oldest people without quarrel or dispute till Wednesday".

Having explained what had happened in the case of John Johnstone, the memorial continued:

"As there appears a fixed resolution and con- spiracy to resist and forcibly obstruct the levy of this usual custom, and as it is of some importance, being, according to the executioner's own account, worth upwards of £13 yearly, the magistrates and Council request the advice of counsel how to act in the business."

The advice the Council received from Crosbie was that the hangman had a clear right to market dues that had been levied by himself and his pre- decessors from time immemorial, and that a more formal procedure should be adopted in any further cases of resistance:

"If the officers, when assisting the hangman in his exactions, are deforced, the deforcers may be

committed to prison and tried criminally by the
magistrates for the deforcement."

The council decided to follow this advice, but
Johnstone was not satisfied just to be released from
jail and "an action was raised in his name for
wrongous imprisonment, and a second, in the shape of
a Declarator, to the effect that the magistrates of
Dumfries had no right in law to let the hangman and
his ladle loose on the public every market-day".

The Town Council Minutes of 14th January,
1782, state:

*"The Magistrates and Councill considering that
in the action at present depending before the Right
Honourable the Lords of Councill and Session at the
instance of John Johnstone in Auchennane against
Nichol Shaw late Dean of this Burgh of Dumfries and
other the Libel contains conclusions for having taken
away or sett aside the dues payable out of the meal
mercat to the Common Executioner.*

*"At the proceeding in which it was objected on
the part of the Magistrates and Councill that they
were not legally cited, but being satisfied that it is
for the interests of the Toun these objections be
waved and the action soon decided.*

*"Therefore the Magistrates and Councill so pass
from these objections and have agreed and resolved
and hereby resolve to sist themselves as a Party to
the said action so far as it contains any conclusions
against them of the Burgh of Dumfries which they
represent and authorise the Touns Lawyer to act
accordingly."*

John Johnstone and the town council thus came
to be involved in protracted litigation before the
Court of Session. Eventually, both actions were dismissed, the council being allowed all its expenses.
"The exact amount of these we do not know," says
one source. "[But] that they were heavy, may be
inferred from this fact, that the extract of the
proceedings... fills hundreds of closely written pages."
Johnstone, being unable to pay, was sent to prison

again. The hangman's dues, needless to say, continued to cause resentment and further attempts were made to deny them to him.

Roger Wilson was succeeded by Joseph Tait on 23rd August, 1785 – and died on 21st September the same year. Tait was imprisoned for debt on 16th December, 1786, and released a month later at the expense of the council. His salary was increased to £10 a year in 1789 after "many complaints that his present salary from the Toun is too small and that he cannot subsist himself and his family thereon it".

He was, by this time, being "in agreed measure deprived of the dues payed to his predecessors by Country people and others who used formerly to bring meal into the public meal mercat", but were now selling it in shops or houses instead. The Council recommended him to take legal action against the traders concerned, but when he tried to do this he was unable to find a writer, i.e., solicitor, willing to act for him.

He petitioned the council for assistance, but the council then decided that it would not "be troubled with any more petitions of the like nature".

Early in 1796 the inhabitants of the town suffered from shortages of food and consequent disturbances. The council issued an address to the farmers of the district requesting them to bring all their spare stocks into the town to be sold in the market-place without delay. The farmers had already signified their willingness to do this, though not without expressing their objections "to the mode in which certain dues were levied at the market". To avert the threat of continued shortage, the council then abolished the hangman's dues, giving him an increase in salary of £2 a year to compensate for his loss.

It is recorded that Roger Wilson's wife committed suicide by hanging herself, though whether this was before or after her husband's death we do not know. His daughters, shortly afterwards, left Dumfries "as the surest way of eschewing the stigma, which, as they perhaps justly imagined, attached to their name". Both are said to have married above their station in life.

Joseph Tait continued as hangman of Dumfries until 1808, when the post was abolished.

At that time his salary was £18 a year, paid in quarterly instalments.

A Miscellany

Robert Wodrow tells us in his *History of the Suffer-ings of the Church of Scotland* (1721-2) that Will-iam Sutherland, hangman of Irvine in 1666, was "very much master of the scriptures, and blameless and pious". He was a poor, self-educated man, who had arrived in Irvine about 5 years earlier, after 4 years of cattle-herding in other parts of Scotland.

It was while he was hangman that he learnt to read, and he tells us in his *Declaration and Examin-ation* (which Wodrow included as an appendix to his book) that, as he became acquainted with the Bible, he "began to scuple to execute any, except that I was clear they deserved to die".

After the Battle of Pentland he was ordered to go to Ayr - the hangman of that town having fled - to execute eight of the rebels. This he refused to do, "because I had heard they were godly Men, who had been opprest by the Bishops, whom I never liked since I loved the Bible". He was taken to Ayr by force, threatened with torture and death, placed in the stocks, and subjected to other forms of hardship and ill-treatment. Yet still he refused.

Finally, one of the rebels, Cornelius Anderson, was prevailed upon to execute the other seven, in return for a pardon for himself. He performed this duty, fortified with brandy, on 27th December, 1666, and executed two more of the rebels in Irvine four

days later. A few days after that he died "in Dis-
traction and great Misery". Sutherland remained in
prison for several weeks and was then released. We
do not know what became of him afterwards.

The following extract from the records of the
Town Council of Wigtown is to be found in the
journal *Notes and Queries:*

Wigtoune, Apryle 15th, 1685.
Councell Extraordinar.
the 91k Day, the bailzie and Councelors present,
having convened John Malroy, hangman, befoir them,
and examined him what was his reason to absent
himself at this tym when ther was employment for
him, he acknowledged he was in the wrong and was
seduced yto; but now acknowledged himself the
tounes ssrt [servant] and promised to byd [abide] be
his service; but aledged that he had noe benefit or
cellarie [salary] for his service and craved to have
som allowance for tyme coming; Which he refered to
the toun councell at ane frequent [early] meiting
efter the provest's returne from Edr.; and in the
meintym the bailzie, with advice and consent of the
Councell, appoints the thessrer [treasurer] to furnish
four shilling Scots [equal to fourpence sterling] ilk
day to the sd. John Malroy dureing his abod in
prissone.

William Andrews, in *Old–Time Punishments*(1890)
says that "if the traditional accounts are to be
credited" the royal burgh of Wigtown had been
granted the privilege of having its own executioner on
the strangest condition:

"The law was that this functionary was himself
to be a criminal under sentence of death, but whose
doom was to be deferred until the advance of age
prevented a continuance of his usefulness, and then
he was to be hanged forthwith."

It is difficult, however, to believe that this is
really true.

In the same book, Andrews quotes the following paragraph from the *Derby Mercury* of 6th April, 1738:

"*Hereford, March 25. - This day Will Summers and Tipping were executed here for housebreaking. At the tree, the hangman was intoxicated with liquor, and supposing that there were three for execution, was going to put one of the ropes round the parson's neck as he stood in the cart, and was with much difficulty prevented by the gaoler from so doing.*"

Another newspaper paragraph relevant to our subject appeared in *Sarah Farley's Bristol Journal* of 2nd May, 1767, and is quoted in *Gloucestershire Notes and Queries* as follows:

"*At the execution of the rioters upon the late special commission at Gloucester, Harris, the common hangman, being at that time in gaol as a party concerned in those outrages, one Evans, of Hampton, was procured to officiate in his stead.*

"*This fellow, last week, committed some trifling theft, for which the justices ordered him to be whipped by his brother hangman, Mr Harris, who told the delinquent that he should severely smart for the reflection he had brought upon the honourable calling to which he had been initiated, and accordingly gave him such a trimming with the cat o'nine tails as must have convinced him that the principles of honour and honesty are essential to that respectable profession.*"

Yet another appeared in *The Times* of 25th December, 1835:

"*At Kirkcudbright, on the 3d current, died Janet Newall, aged 84 years. She was the last of the family of John Newall, who held the respectable situation of hangman in the town of Kirkcudbright for many years, and who never had an opportunity of exercising the important duties of his office excepting on one solitary occasion, in the year 1750. Besides Janet, the hangman had two other children, Elizabeth and William. Elizabeth, commonly called*

'Lizzie Newall', was a well-known character in Kirkcudbright."

The *Edinburgh Evening Courant* of 4th July, 1772, contained an advertisement for a hangman in Haddington, stating:

"He will have £3 Sterling of wages yearly, a free house, new cloathes; and his perquisites in meal, wool and calling of fish, greens, and other commodities, are very considerable."

The *Aberdeen Journal* 8th June, 1789, had a similar advertisement for a hangman in Elgin:

"He will have a free house, and about two acres of land, a number of perquisites payable out of the commodities sold in town, and a considerable salary."

In this case, *The Times* of 29th June reported that nobody could be found to fill the post, adding that it was, in any case, a sinecure, as there had not been an execution in Elgin "within our memory".

An extract from the Stirling Town Council Minutes for 2nd February, 1771, reads:

"The Councill Considering, That John Rankine the present Staffman, Is not only upon Occasions when necessity Calls unable to execute his Office, But also that he and his wife keep a Bad house in the Night time by entertaining Tinkers and Vagabonds & having quarrels with them to the great nuisance & disturbance of the Neighbourhood, They therefore Dismiss him as Staffman And appoint the treasurer to give him Ten shillings Sterling money for paying the Expence of Carrying him & his Wife to Glasgow or elsewhere."

Rankine was the last hangman of Stirling whose name is known to us, and there is no earlier reference to him in the council minutes.

The last known reference to a Stirling hangman appears in an entry in the Burgh Accounts for 1789-90, in which we find the burgh jailer being paid £4.19s. "for Staffman from 1 Nov. 1789 to 17 May 1790."

Edinburgh's most celebrated hangman was undoubtedly John Dalgleish. A former waterman, he was appointed on 25th July, 1722, when his predecessor, Donald Sutherland, was "suspended" for "several misdemeanours".

It was Dalgleish who officiated in the Grassmarket on 2nd September, 1724, when Margaret Dickson, a native of Musselburgh, was hanged for the murder of her illegitimate child, but found to be still alive after being cut down from the gallows and given to her friends for burial.

It was also he who executed Andrew Wilson, a smuggler convicted of robbery at an excise office, on 14th April, 1736, when a disturbance led to the Town Guard – an armed force primarily responsible for the preservation of public order – firing into the crowds and killing a number of people.

Dalgleish remained hangman for 26 years, inflicting a variety of punishments. The Edinburgh Treasurer's Accounts for 1734-5 show a number of payments made to him, some referring to him by name. One entry, dated 10th September, 1735, reads:

Paid the Lockman his fees for two
  whippings,   0 6 8
Paid Ditto for hanging James Broun
  at Galalee,   1 2 2
Paid Ditto for ropes,   0 5 0
Paid Ditto for Barrel Salt, etc.,   0 2 0

The London Journal of 9th August, 1729, contains a report from Edinburgh, dated 31st July, as follows:

"Yesterday, by Warrant of the Magistrates, Hair-Merchant who had carried on a Practice of cheating the Wigmakers with Wool mixt with Horse Hair, and selling it for human Hair, was imprisoned, and his Cargo burnt at the Cross by the Common Hangman."

The Caledonian Mercury of 29th March, 1742, reported:

"That Day [26th]... a Sedan or Chair, with all

its Accoutrements, was burnt at the Cross by the Common Executioner, having been stopt at the Netherbow-port with a dead Corpse in it some Weeks ago. "

In 1746 Dalgleish had another strange duty – that of carrying the defeated Young Pretender's standard in procession through the city.

It is also known that he was paid a salary of £5 a year for his services as dempster, in addition to his salary and perquisites as hangman.

Robert Chambers says that Dalgleish once remarked, in speaking of the whippings he inflicted: "I lay on the lash according to my conscience."

The Caledonian Mercury of 18th July, 1748, reported his demise four days earlier:

"Thursday last died at his House in the Foot of the Fishmarket Close, betwixt 70 and 80 Years of Age, honest John Dalgleish, Dempster to the Court of Justiciary, and final Executioner of the Law for the City of Edinburgh, and on Friday Night the Corpse, escorted by the City Guard, was interred by the Chimney Sweepers in the Gray-Friars Church-Yard. "

The newspaper commented that Dalgleish "was a Man all along famed for being *conscientious* to a Degree in the Exercise of his Office".

The house in the Fishmarket Close – "a small wretched-looking house", according to Chambers – was provided by the magistrates for whoever happened to be currently in office. It continued to be the Edinburgh hangman's home until the following century.

In *A History of Capital Punishment* by John Laurence, we find the story of Roger Gray, a seventeenth century Exeter hangman, who is said to have hanged his own brother. We also find, in the same book, the tale of John Crosland, a horse-thief, also of the seventeenth century, who is said to have become

hangman of Derby after hanging his father and elder
brother (who had been convicted with him) in return
for a pardon. No sources of any sort are given for
the information about these characters and no
reliable sources have been discovered during the
researches for this book. One suspects that they are
both of fictional origin.

At the Somerset Assizes held at Bridgwater on
1st-3rd August, 1785, one Thomas Woodham was
brought to trial for assaulting and robbing another
man of 1s.6d on the highway "near Bath Easton". He
was convicted, sentenced to death, and ordered for
execution on 10th August.

Woodham, aged 69, was the hangman of
Gloucester. We do not know the date on which his
crime was committed, but it is known that he
returned to Gloucester before being apprehended, and
carried out an execution there on 18th July.

The General Evening Post of 13th-16th August
says that he had previously been tried in Gloucester
on a number of occasions, though without giving any
details of these trials.

On his way to the gallows, with five other
prisoners, Woodham expressed regret at having been
unable to "dispose of the two or three convicts who
remained to be executed in his own county".

The six executions were carried out from the
back of a cart, all of the sufferers behaving "in a
manner becoming to their unhappy situations". Three
of them had to be hanged a second time, the ropes
having slipped from their necks at the first attempt.
Woodham, however, did not suffer this additional
misfortune.

Wales seems to have had a lot more difficulty
than either England or Scotland in finding people to
carry out executions.

An entry in the *Calendar of Treasury Books &
Papers* for 8th June, 1743, records:

"*A petition read from Lewis Merrick, late*

under-sheriff of Merioneth, for repayment of his expenses, &c., in procuring a person out of England to hang the convict David Williams in Wales. Nothing done. "

Another entry, for 9th April, 1745, concerns a petition from the sheriff of Anglesey for the reimbursement of £60 "for his extraordinary expenses for an executioner and in erecting a pillory."

In March, 1769, one Edward Edwards was convicted of burglary and felony before the Court of Great Sessions for the County of Flint. Sentenced to death, he was to be hanged "on next Monday Fortnight the 10th April". However, Flintshire had no hangman and the under-sheriff, Ralph Griffith, believed that it would be "almost impossible" to find any native of that country to hang another. The execution had to be postponed while enquiries were made in Liverpool and Shrewsbury in the hope of finding an Englishman to carry it out. This proved to be both troublesome and expensive.

Before long, a man in Shropshire agreed to perform the duty. He was given five guineas in part payment and set out for Flintshire in the company of Griffith's men, but on the road he deserted his companions, taking the money (about sixteen times the value of the goods which Edwards was convicted of having stolen) with him. They returned home without an executioner.

The execution was finally carried out by a fellow prisoner named John Babington about two months after it had originally been due to take place. Babington was paid six guineas for serving as hangman and his wife the same sum for persuading him to do it!

Afterwards, Griffith calculated the expenses which had been incurred in connection with the execution as follows:

Travelling & other expenses	£15.10s.0d.
Part payment to Shropshire man	£ 5. 5s.0d.
Expenses of his escorts	£ 4.10s.0d.
To Babington	£ 6. 6s.0d.
To Babington's wife	£ 6. 6s.0d.
Materials & labour for gallows	£ 4.12s.0d.
Cart, coffin & burial	£ 2.10s.0d.
Additional expenses (minimum)	£ 5. 0s.0d.
Total	£49.19s.0d.

His petition for reimbursement was published in *Lloyds Evening Post* of 19th-21st June, 1769.

The hangman's house at Stirling.

Brunskill & his Mate

William Brunskill was about 43 years old at the time of his appointment as hangman of London and had been assistant to Edward Dennis for at least 11 years. He seems to have had no regular assistant himself until John Langley, a labourer aged about 24, was appointed about 1790. Langley was to continue working with him for the next 24 years and then take over the post of hangman when Brunskill was no longer able to carry out his duties.

The late eighteenth and early nineteenth centuries were times of considerable change for all of our hangmen. The number of capital offences remained at its height: there were about 200 according to some estimates and 350 according to others, the variation being caused by loose wording in some of the statutes. Nevertheless, the number of executions continued to decline and more and more towns were relying upon the hangmen of other towns, rather than continuing to employ one of their own.

There were changes, too, in both the places and the apparatus of execution, the common or marketplace giving way to the front or roof of the prison, the gallows-tree to the scaffold.

At Newgate the collapsible platform was soon replaced by a platform of a different sort - one which, at an execution in 1797, "accidentally gave way, and precipitated the two clergymen and the executioners (though with little hurt), to the ground; and the unhappy sufferers into eternity, before the caps were drawn over their faces".

Though the 'Tyburn Fair' had been discontinued, executions still caused much public excitement and disorder. When three culprits were hanged (all for murder) on 23rd February, 1807, the pressure of the crowd was so great that "some fell, and others tumbled over them; till there were two or three heaps of persons in this situation, all struggling with each other to extricate themselves".

"It was full half an hour before effectual assistance could be given. Besides several persons who were taken away in carts, desperately hurt, the following is a statement of those killed or wounded. In St Bartholomew's Hospital, dead, men, 24; women, 3. Wounded, men, 12; women, 3. In St Sepulchre's church, 2 boys dead. At the White Swan wine-vaults, 1 youth dead. Total, 30 dead, 15 wounded."

The declining number of executions, to Brunskill, was a source of dissatisfaction. In *The Times* of 30th January, 1794, we find:

"A petition from William Brunskill (commonly called Jack Ketch) was presented to the Court [of Aldermen, stating] that he was the public executioner, and on that account could not get any other employment; that he was obliged to keep an [assistant], though his allowance was so small and his income so [trifling], as to be insufficient to maintain himself and family, and praying relief. - The Court referred the same to the Sheriffs."

The result of this petition is unknown. It is possible that it was at this stage that the London hangman started to receive a wage of one guinea a week. If not, then Brunskill's hardship must have increased during 1794, for in that year there were only seven executions in London, compared with 16 in 1793 and 92 in 1787.

Thereafter, the number of executions rose and fell, but the trend was always downwards until the

shrievalty of Sir Richard Phillips in 1807-8 when
there was not a single one. At this point - or so it
has been claimed - Brunskill refused to inflict
whippings, claiming that his post was now "worth
nothing at all". "I used to get a few suits of clothes
after a sessions, but for many months I have had no
job but whipping, and that puts nothing in a man's
pocket," he complained.

The complaint was not altogether justified, for
by now he certainly was receiving a guinea a week
and to the sheriff this seemed sufficient as the post
had become "almost a sinecure". Brunskill protested
that he had to pay his assistant half a guinea a week
and had only "a hanging job now and then in the
country, where there's few in my line" to save him
from ruination.

Sir Richard thereupon agreed that Brunskill
should be paid half a guinea extra a week.

When Phillips left office the hangings started
again; occasionally, in the years that followed, there
were six or seven prisoners hanged at a time. In
general, though, the numbers were much smaller than
they had been in Brunskill's first years as hangman
and gave him little cause for celebration.

Among the prisoners executed during Brunskill's
long period of office there were Joseph Wall, a
former Governor of Goree (Senegal), in 1802 for a
murder committed nearly 20 years earlier; Captain
John Sutherland in 1809 for the murder of his negro
servant; and John Bellingham in 1812 for the murder
of Spencer Perceval, Chancellor of the Exchequer.
Christian Murphy, a coiner, was burnt in 1789;
Colonel Despard, a traitor, and a number of associates were hanged and beheaded in 1803, the decapit-
ations being carried out by a masked man who was
reputed to be a surgeon. At a multiple execution in
1814, one of the culprits rebounded from the rope
and landed back on the scaffold floor, so that the
hangman had to push him down again.

In 1814 Brunskill suffered "a paralytic stroke",

which left him "totally unfit for any bodily exertion". He remained nominally the hangman until the following year, but Langley carried out his duties, with James Botting, an illiterate man, acting as his assistant. Brunskill's formal resignation was contained in a petition to the Court of Aldermen read on 9th May, 1815, in which he stated that he was now 72 years old and had "served the Office of Executioner upwards of forty years". The Court granted him a pension of 15s. a week.

Probably the first execution carried out by Langley and Botting was that of four Malays, who were hanged at Execution Dock on 15th December, 1814, for a murder committed on the high seas. As always in such cases, there was a procession through the streets, the hangman and his assistant riding in the cart with drawn cutlasses. In this particular case, however, the condemned were also accompanied by two interpreters. The hangings were carried out on a temporary gallows.

After all his service as assistant to Brunskill, Langley was only to be hangman in his own right for two years, for he died on 27th April, 1817, leaving a wife, Elizabeth, and three young children. His career, in fact, had been so much overshadowed by Brunskill's that when his widow petitioned the Court of Aldermen for financial help she was referred to in the Court's minutes as "Widow of John Langley, late Assistant to the Public Hangman".

Langley had been unwell for some time prior to his death. *Bell's Weekly Messenger* of 4th May, 1817, records that he had received treatment at the London Hospital as an out-patient at first, but died an inmate.

His wife's petition, dated 13th May, said that she was suffering great hardship; that "through the unfortunate occupation of her Husband, she [was] now totally precluded from getting her Living and from the general contempt which his calling [had] brought on her she [was] now with three Children thrown on

the World without her Friend to give her the least
assistance". She begged the court to provide not only
financial help, but also an education for her children,
in order to prevent them suffering "unmerited disdain
from their father's calling".

The court, however, resolved only "that the
Sheriffs be recommended to pay the said Elizabeth
Langley the Salary which would have been due to her
Husband at Midsummer next".

Old Ned

Edward Barlow, commonly called 'Old Ned', was hang man of Lancaster from about 1781 until his death in 1812. During that time he carried out 131 executions, many of them on Lancaster Common, but there is no record of his inflicting other types of punishment. He was a well-known and much-disliked character.

Joseph Hall, author of *Lancaster Castle; its History and Associations* (1843), says that he was reputed to be "as great a villain as any man ever put to death".

"From information we learn that this man led a wretched life; there were very few houses into which he was permitted to enter; he was ever the butt of scorn for all persons; many times he was seriously abused; often pelted with missiles of the foulest description; and not unfrequently was he rolled in the mud, and as often much worse treated in a nameless manner; yet this wretch maintained his horrible post, with little intermission, during a period of thirty years."

Barlow, a Welshman, was born in 1736. There are few references to him in the surviving newspapers and official records and Hall's brief sketch is by no means reliable. We know nothing about his income and perquisites (if he had any) and Hall's claim that the hangman was "guilty of nearly every vile act; was many times convicted, and twice sentenced to transportation for life" is a great exaggeration.

We do, however, know of one occasion when Barlow was in trouble with the law for stealing a horse. This occurred in 1806, when he appeared at the March Assizes in Lancaster, charged with "stealing a chestnut coloured gelding belonging to Peter Wright of North Meols", having been committed to prison on 28th December the previous year. The charge was proved against him and 'Old Ned' was reported to have remarked, on leaving the dock: "All this comes of a man getting out of his line!"

He was 69 years old at the time and had already hanged 84 criminals: though sentenced to death, he was afterwards reprieved on condition of serving ten years' imprisonment in Lancaster Castle. He was to remain a prisoner for the rest of his life, being brought out of jail whenever there was an execution to be carried out.

The circumstances of his confinement are not known, but it may be supposed that arrangements were made for him to be protected from the other prisoners, for he would otherwise have suffered greatly at their hands.

The last person to be hanged on Lancaster Common was James Case, a surgeon convicted of forgery, in 1799 – when, according to Hall, an un-successful attempt was made to save the prisoner's life by means of a small pipe inserted into his throat. Thereafter, Lancaster's place of execution was at the back of the Castle. It was there that eleven people were hanged together after the March Assizes of 1801, the drop being "so badly managed that the toes of some of the unfortunate culprits touched the scaffold".

Barlow, it seems, was unperturbed by incidents like this. "His profession (strange to tell) was to him a subject of pride and boasting, and he would often talk of the *neatness* in which he would *execute* it," says one of his obituary notices. And, according to Hall "[he] often used to boast he had 'rid the world of many a rogue, and saved the life of one honest man'; he having, on one occasion, rescued a very worthy individual from a watery grave".

He died in the Castle at the age of 76 on 9th December, 1812, and was buried the following day at St Mary's Parish Church, Lancaster.

It is probable that he was the last hangman to be employed regularly in Lancaster and that, after his death, the town relied upon the services of the hangmen of York or London.

THE PROCESSION
OF
J A M E S   M A C N A M A R A,
From the New Bayley Prison,
Who is to be executed on the Great Hill, on Kersal Moor,
Sept. 11, 1790.
Four Sheriff's Officers.
Eight Javelin Men, four and four.

Two Javelin Men.	Cart	Two Javelin Men.
Two Sheriff's Officers.	with the	Two Sheriff's Officers.
Two Javelin Men.	Culprit.	Two Javelin Men.

Eight Javelin Men, four and four.
Four Sheriff's Officers.
Under Sheriff.
Clergyman.
Magistrates' Coach, &c., with Mr. Bayley, Mr. Milne, and Mr. Fox.
Deputy Constable.
Boroughreeves of Manchester and Salford.
Constables of Manchester and Salford.
Beadles in cloaks and caps.
Special Constables, four and four.
Gentlemen.
Servants.
The Bells at all the Churches will be tolled.

Plan of procession to the gallows in 1790.
From 'The Reliquary', v.IX.

A Man from the Hulks

At the Lent Assizes in York in 1793 William Curry, a labourer from Thirsk in the North Riding, was brought to trial for the capital crime of sheep--stealing. It was alleged that on 13th December previously, in the village of Romanby (also in the North Riding), he had stolen "three Ewe Sheep of the Price of three pounds of the Goods and Chattels of one William Smith", a Northallerton innkeeper.

Curry, otherwise known as William Wilkinson, pleaded guilty and was sentenced to death - a sentence afterwards commuted to seven years' transportation.

Two further charges of a similar nature had also been made against him: one that he had stolen "seven Hog Sheep of the price of four pounds" in the Parish of Easingwold on 17th November, 1792; the other that he had stolen "one Ewe Sheep of the price of Six Shillings and five Hog Sheep of the price of three pounds" in the same parish the following day. Neither of these charges was pursued, presumably because he had admitted the offence in Romanby.

Curry was not transported: instead, he served his term aboard the hulks in Woolwich.

The hulks, or prison-ships, had been introduced in 1776 after transportation to the American colonies was brought to an end by the War of Independence. The convicts, chained by the leg in pairs, were kept

at hard labour, dredging the river between Woolwich
and Barking. The scheme remained in operation for a
long time after the opening of the Botany Bay
settlement in Australia.

Curry survived his term and was discharged
from the hulks on 18th March, 1800. Returning to
Yorkshire, he was soon in trouble again, for on 15th
August he was "charged upon the oaths of Thomas
Severs, Joseph Pardoe, and John Jackson, with
stealing, on... the 31st day of July last, or early the
following morning, five ewe sheep, the property of
the said Thomas Severs, from out of a field in the
occupation of the said Thomas Severs, situate in the
township of Heworth, in the North-Riding". He was
committed to prison to await trial. The five ewes
were together valued at £12.

At the Lent Assizes the following year, Curry
- whose age is given as 31 in a *Calendar of Felons*
- admitted the offence and was once more sentenced
to death. This time the sentence was commuted to
one of 14 years' transportation - and somehow this
became changed to one of 14 years' imprisonment in
York Castle.

Within the next year or so the post of hangman for the City and County became vacant and the
jailer of York Castle, "by the terms of his bond to
the Sheriff of the County", had the task of finding
somebody to fill it. Curry, who was "under considerable obligations" to the jailer, was prevailed upon to
accept it, and was appointed to the post at the
Summer Assizes, 1802. His release from prison took
place in 1814 or 1815.

Curry remained hangman of Yorkshire for about
33 years and was known as 'Mutton Curry' in consequence of his convictions. He carried out several
dozen executions in York alone, putting to death no
fewer than fourteen people in one day in 1813; he
also travelled to other parts of the north of England
when a hangman was needed there.

"It is generally acknowledged, that he filled

the situation with sufficient ability," said one contemporary newspaper, "but it is to be much regretted
that, whilst preparing the final noose for his unfortunate victims, *gin* was apt to provide a *snare* to him,
and that he could never be induced to adjust a
hempen cord without an undue allowance of *blue
thread."*

This proclivity led to an astonishing performance at the execution of William Brown, a robber,
outside York's city jail on 14th April, 1821. It was
York's second execution of the day, that of Michael
Shaw (another robber) had taken place about an hour
and a quarter earlier at the Castle (the county jail)
- at which time the executioner "appeared quite
sober".

*"Unfortunately for Curry Wilkinson, in pro-
ceeding from the County execution which he had
conducted with his usual propriety, to the place of
execution for the City, he was recognised by the
populace, who were posting with unsatiated appetites
from one feast of death to another: by a strange
inconsistency, they hustled and insulted the executioner to such a degree during the whole of his walk,
that he arrived nearly exhausted; and with nerves
quite inadequate to the task he had still to perform.*

*"Under these circumstances, it was, that he
unfortunately applied the stimulus of spirits, which a
sterner and more relentless character would not have
required."*

Reaching the city jail drunk, he began fixing
his rope to the overhead beam of the scaffold with a
jocularity which hardly befitted the occasion. In spite
of a heavy and continual fall of rain, there was an
unusually large number of spectators, and 'Mutton
Curry' amused himself at one stage by shaking the
halter at them and calling out, "Some of you come
up and I'll try it!"

Then, when the prisoner was brought on to the
scaffold and the religious preparations began, his
manner changed to one of "heart-sickening officious-

ness". It soon became clear that he was unable to perform his duty properly, for he had difficulty even in pulling the cap over the condemned man's face. He then discovered that the rope was too short, so the proceedings were held up while he lengthened it.

After that, he tried several times to put the halter round the prisoner's neck, but each time succeeded only in removing the cap from his face. The spectators raised their voices in horror, calling upon the under-sheriff to intervene, until finally, with the assistance of the jailer and one of the sheriff's officers, the hanging was carried out. Curry was after wards "assailed by the populace with shouts of execration, and several called out, 'Hang him - hang Jack Ketch - he's drunk.'"

"On his return home, he was repeatedly knocked down and beaten by the mob," *The Yorkshire Gazette* recorded.

This was not the only occasion on which Curry bungled his work. In September the same year, on carrying out a multiple execution, he stood too close to the platform, so that "when the bolt was pulled out, he fell along with the malefactors, and received some severe bruises" - to the delight of the spectators.

Despite these incidents, however, he remained hangman of York until November, 1835, or thereabouts, when he retired to the parish workhouse of Thirsk.

He did not carry out the execution of Charles Batty (for attempted murder) on 2nd April, 1836, as has been stated: this was carried out by "a convict who has been confined during the last twelve months in the Castle, and who has been induced to take upon himself this revolting occupation".

Nor did he die "soon after" this event, as has also be claimed, for the Thirsk burial register (in the North Yorkshire County Archives Department) records the following interment in 1841:

"Mar 10 William Curry of Thirsk, aged 76."

The entry makes no mention of Thirsk Union Workhouse, as might be expected. Also, the age given does not correspond with the evidence of the March, 1801 *Calendar of Felons* which suggests that Curry would only have been about 71 in 1841, but such discrepancies are by no means uncommon.

There is no other entry during the period 1836-41 that could refer to the subject of the present chapter; so it is reasonable to suppose that the one in question is indeed that of the retired hangman. If it is not, then we do not know what became of him.

The convict who executed Charles Batty was, in all likelihood, James Coates, who had been convicted of larceny at the Summer Assizes the previous year and sentenced to seven years' transportation.

If so, then this man held the office of hangman for the next four years, for in April, 1840, we find that Nathaniel Howard was appointed to it, "Coates, the burglar... having escaped from the Castle". Nathaniel Howard was a coal-porter.

The Coming of Calcraft

At some stage during the tenure of office of William Brunskill, or soon afterwards, the post of assistant hangman became officially recognised, its occupant being paid his wages by the sheriff or under-sheriff. It would seem that at that stage the wages of the finisher of the law and his assistant were settled at one guinea and half a guinea a week respectively.

James Botting, at any rate, did receive half a guinea as assistant to John Langley and within a few months of his appointment petitioned the Court of Aldermen, stating that this was "inadequate to his own support much less that of his family", and that "the unpleasant nature of your Petitioners employment and from the prejudice of the public against any person fulfilling it and dischargeing its duties renders it impossible... to gain another regular employment to derive any additional means of support". The Court referred the petition to the sheriffs for consideration, but no increase in wages resulted.

When Langley died, Botting took his place, carrying out his first execution in that capacity on 2nd May, 1817. A Henry Small afterwards petitioned the Court, saying that he had helped Botting at that execution and praying that he might be appointed his assistant. The Court decided that an assistant hangman was no longer needed.

Eighteen months later a second petition from Botting was presented to the Court of Aldermen, detailing various grievances. In it he stated that his predecessors had "always received some small fees on the Executions from the Undertakers or Friends of the Criminals executed, also the privelege of rubbing of persons afflicted with wens for which it was usual to receive two shillings and six pence for each person";*that he himself had enjoyed these fees and perquisites until a few weeks earlier, and that they were now denied to him "by order of the Honourable Committee".

He stated too, that John Langley "at the time of the Sessions received two shillings per day for his attendance whereas your Petitioner has the duty of two persons to attend there being no settled Assistant Executioner as was always before and your Petitioner has only one shilling per day for his attendance".

He prayed for the Court's "consideration" in respect of these losses of income, and reminded them that he was unable to obtain any other employment "in consequence of his Situation as Executioner".

He then went on to say that he was often in great danger as a result of his work, suggesting that he might be given "the power of a Peace Officer", which would enable him to "protect himself in all Cases of Public assault" and "enable him to check the attempts of the lower order against him".

The Court referred the petition to its Committee for General Purposes. Four months later "[the] Committee appointed to consider of all matters relating to the Gaols of this City" reported that its members had considered the petition and were "of opinion that this Court should not interfere therein". The report was "well liked and approved".

*The bodies of hanged criminals were widely believed to have curative powers, and many people paid for the privilege of having parts of their own bodies rubbed against them.

Botting was a native of Brighton, where his father had owned "some small property at the back of West Field Lodge, immediately to the west of the bottom of Cannon Place, and known as Botting's Rookery, from its being the resort of tramps of the lowest order," says John Ackerson Erredge's *History of Brighthelmston* (1862).

His petitions, drawn up by a professional pen-man, show that while in the service of the Court of Aldermen he lived in Shoreditch.

He was hangman for only about three years, following an even shorter period as assistant hangman, yet it is suggested in one of his obituaries that he executed no fewer than 175 criminals.

"He did his work without uttering a word to the 'party', as he used to call the unfortunate being doomed to pass through his hands", the same source tells us.

It was during his incumbency that a new custom began: that of paying the hangman his wages over the door of Newgate Prison "in conformity with the feelings of the turnkeys".

Botting retired from his post "in consequence of paralysis", probably early in 1820. Four years later he was in prison for debt. The Court of Aldermen then granted him a pension of 5s. per week and at the same time instructed the City Solicitor to obtain his discharge.

Botting was succeeded as hangman by James Foxen, who had been assisting him, however irregularly, since about 1818. Foxen, who was called Foxton in the newspapers, was in turn helped by Thomas Cheshire (sometimes called Jack Cheshire).

It was Foxen and Cheshire, if their obituary notices are to be believed, who hanged the five Cato Street Conspirators for high treason on 1st May, 1820, in a performance which Cheshire afterwards described as "a miracle of skill, steadiness and tact". The prisoners were afterwards decapitated by a masked man - the same man who had beheaded

Despard and his associates, according to *The Morning Chronicle's* account.

Thereafter, Cheshire continued to work with Foxen for 8 years, though how he was remunerated we do not know.

Foxen, like Botting, was illiterate, as we know from a petition he addressed to the Court of Aldermen, dated 13th May, 1828. We also learn from this that he was aged "60 and upwards" and living at No.19, Booth Street, Hoxton.

He carried out executions in many parts of the country outside London, including that of William Corder, the 'Red Barn' murderer, at Bury St Edmunds on 11th August, 1828. A contemporary account of this case tells us a little more about him.

"After the executioner had fixed the rope to the beam, and was busy in tying what he calls the 'mysterious knot', it was suggested to him that he had left too much for what is technically called 'the fall', in consequence of which he reluctantly took part of it up, and it was quite evident that Mister Ketch did not relish this interference with his public functions."

Foxen, in fact, was disconcerted enough by this interference to "[precipitate] the felon into eternity before the signal was given".

"After the execution was over, Foxton expressed his chagrin at having been interrupted in the performance of his professional duty. He said, 'I never like to be meddled with, because I always study the subjects which come under my hands, and, according as they are tall or short, heavy or light, I accommodate them with the fall. No man in England has had so much experience as me, or knows how to do his duty better.'

"In the after part of the day, this public functionary visited the corpse in the Shire Hall, for the purpose of claiming Corder's trowsers, when he pointed to his handywork upon the neck of the criminal, and asked, exultingly, whether he had not

'done the job in a masterly manner'."

Foxen's petition, three months earlier, had stated that he was "in a very infirm state of health and not able to perform the duties allotted to him by the Sheriffs", and prayed that he would be granted "the Pension as the former Executioners have had".

It seems that he was still in office when he died on 14th February the following year.

As for Cheshire, he was married and lodged in Bell Court, Giltspur Street, conveniently near to New-gate Prison. *The Heroes of the Guillotine and Gallows* (1868) tells us that he "used to wear always a snuff-brown coat reaching down to his heels". Sometimes he carried out executions on his own.

One of his contemporaries, writing over 30 years later in *Notes and Queries* says that he was known by the nick-name of 'Old Cheese' and goes on to record his disgust as follows:

"Horrible stories are yet told of the fiendish delight, even when a feeble old man, which he seemed to take in his wretched office. The basilisk gleam of his eye, the stealthy cat-like clutch with which he pounced upon his victim - foh! I saw Cheshire once, and, while memory holds its seat, I never will forget the occasion."

Another account states:

"When Cheshire officiated at Horsemonger-lane Gaol [in Surrey], he was obliged to perform the whole ceremony, and the manner in which he performed part of it was truly appalling. After the bolt is pulled, it is usual for the functionary to take hold of the body, in order to render the passage to the other world as quick as possible. Cheshire, the moment the pangs became visible, made a rush at the malefactor, and swung for some minutes with him, as if a certain delight were communicated by the idea of ushering a soul into eternity."

But it was also said of him that he "always gave courage with a whisper while making a neck ready for the start".

When Foxen died it was announced that Cheshire was his successor, but a few weeks later, on 5th April, 1829, *The Observer* and *Bell's Life in London* reported that a man named Calcraft had been appointed hangman "in the room of Foxton", so either Cheshire had been passsed over or London now had *two* hangmen, both presumably being paid a guinea a week over the prison door.

Cheshire, at any rate, was recognised as *the* hangman, or at least as *one of the hangmen*, till his death in 1830.

In August, 1829, an incident took place outside Cheshire's home that led to his wife making two appearances in court at the Guildhall. *The Times* of 20th August reported:

" *Ann Cheshire,* the wife of the common hangman, was brought up for re-examination, charged with assaulting four children.

"A poor woman named Cahill, who lodges in the same house with the prisoner, in a court in Giltspur-street, had complained that the prisoner came home drunk on Saturday afternoon, and after knocking two of her children down while they were playing in the court, picked them up and threw them down an area into a cellar ten feet deep, and then flung two other children upon them. Neither of the four, however, were seriously hurt, and as the prisoner had suffered 40 hours' imprisonment, the complainant did not wish to press any charge.

"Mr Alderman ANSLEY said, this was such an outrageous act, that he could not allow it to be passed over in that way, and he remanded the prisoner for 48 hours more, that she might have some punishment, and that the mother of the other children might come forward to complain, if she chose.

"Yesterday, when the prisoner was brought up, Mrs Cahill was in the same forgiving temper.

"Old Mr Cheshire, assuming an over-kind good-natured manner, assured the Alderman she was remarkably attached to children, and gave them many

*halfpence, and it was because she had no halfpence
to give them on Saturday, and they therefore bawled
after her 'Jack Ketch', that she became irritated,
and accidentally knocked them down the cellar.*

"Notwithstanding her protestations, the alderman would not part with her until she had given
sureties for her future good behaviour."

Cheshire's last days were haunted by his fear
of body-snatching, of which there was a resurgence
in the early nineteenth century. No longer able to
snatch corpses at places of execution, gangs had
started to remove them from freshly-dug graves,
acquiring for themselves the appelation of 'Resurrect-
ionists' or 'Resurrection Men'.

The Times   of 13th July, 1830, reporting his
death, said:

"Cheshire always had the greatest terror of the
resurrection-men, and was often told, by those of
that class who at last fell within his clutches, that
the 'trade' would have him at any risk when his
mortal career should be terminated. His last words
were upon this subject.

"He requested that his blessing might be given
to Mr Wontner, the Governor of Newgate, and that
gentleman's family, accompanied by the solemn
entreaty that his remains should be buried in Newgate. It has, however, been thought proper to give
him 'Christian burial', and that St Sepulchre's church
yard shall receive the body of the most ingenius of
executioners.

"His wife, in the apprehension that an attempt
would be made to steal the corpse, actually slept
with her head upon the cold arm of the deceased,
and on Friday night she was awakened by the noise
of some of the 'snatchers', who attempted to gain an
entrance at the two-pair of stairs window."

James Botting, in the meantime, had moved
back to Brighton, where he lived on his pension for
the rest of his life.

He was a well-known character there, and

moved about the streets with a chair, which he used as a crutch as well as a seat, but, says Erredge, "he always appeared isolated from the world, as no grade of society seemed ambitious of the acquaintance of Jack Ketch". He lived in lodgings, and, towards the end of his life, became feeble and nervous through illness, so that "it was with much difficulty [that] he walked across the floor of the room in which he reposed".

"Of late his sleep had been disturbed by visions of certain scenes in which he had performed a prominent character, and in which all the 'parties' moved on before his imagination in a more frightful cavalcade than the witches conjured up before the eyes of *Macbeth*", it was reported after his death.

"He used to dream that 175 'parties' with their night-caps on, and their heads inclined to the left shoulders, were moving before him, and he frequently said, in speaking of the horrors of his sleep, D--n their eyes, if they'd only hold up their heads and take off their night-caps, [I wouldn't] care a blaust about 'em."

He was, nonetheless, much excited at the impending execution of James Greenacre, a murderer, some months before his own death, as the clock struck eight on the morning of 2nd May, 1837, he called out from his bed: "That's the time o'day! I'm blessed if he ain't a-coming out to nap it!"

On 1st October the former hangman "went off without saying a word, and so nobody never said a word to him".

His landlord and landlady sent a letter to the hall-keeper at the Guildhall, asking that, as he had died poor, "the Corporation would be so good as to grant the price of a shell and prayers for their departed brother".

The Police Committee considered the letter and directed the hall-keeper to send the couple £2.

Neither a Sampson nor a Hercules

Thomas Young, the last Glasgow hangman to hold an official post, was appointed to office on 10th December, 1814. A native of Berwickshire and a former soldier in the Berwickshire Regiment, he had, since arriving in Glasgow, worked as a labourer. He was able to produce impressive character references and the city magistrates had an indenture drawn up, binding him to occupy the post for the rest of his life. During the next 23 years he was to carry out over 70 executions, 56 of them in Glasgow, and to become well-known all over Scotland.

In signing his indenture, Young undertook to "[put] into full execution the Sentences of the... Magistrates and their Successors in Office, and the Sentences of the Lords Commissioners of Justiciary appointed to be put in force by the Magistrates of Glasgow, whether the same be capital or shall consist in whipping Criminals, putting them in the pillory, or in the Stocks, or exposing them upon the platform; and in General... to perform every duty of the above description, which the Magistrates may have occasion, from time to time, to direct".

He undertook, in addition to inflicting punishment upon offenders, to work as a labourer "during the usual Working hours" under the direction of the Superintendent of Works, doing "such work as the said Superintendent shall prescribe to him, it being

understood however that his said services shall be
confined to the public Offices and Jail, such as
carrying coals, putting on fires, Cleaning pavements
on the out & insides of the Jail and Wards thereof
and doing any other such Work about the premises as
the said Superintendent may from time to time
direct".

He undertook, furthermore, to live quietly,
soberly and "regularly in all respects".

For their own part, the magistrates bound
themselves and their successors to pay him a salary
of £50 a year (30s. every Friday and the amount out-
standing every 10th June and 10th December), with a
guinea for each execution, and to provide him with a
free house within the prison grounds, together with
coal and candles, and a pair of shoes twice a year -
"it being understood that the said Thomas Young
shall provide all his other Cloths, at his own
expence".

It was not the first time that the magistrates
had insisted upon their hangman living quietly, soberly
and "regularly". On 16th April, 1803, an advertisement appeared in the *Glasgow Courier* as follows:

*"Wanted, for the City of Glasgow, an Execut-
ioner. The bad character of the person who last held
the office having brought on it a degree of discredit
which it by no means deserves, the Magistrates are
determined to accept of none but a sober well--
behaved man. The emoluments are considerable."*

The fellow they appointed to the post then was
one Archibald McArthur, nicknamed 'Buffy', who was
to be hangman for about ten years. At the time of
his appointment he was about 30 years old, "about 5
feet 2 inches in height, stout and rotund in body,
with short bandy-legs, and a big bullet-shaped head,
with a florid bloated countenance, and thick lips,"
says one source. He was said to be "a good natured
inoffensive creature".

We do not know whether he fulfilled his
obligation to be sober and well-behaved, but his wife

was "an inveterate tippler". He died in the Glasgow Infirmary, where his only child, a hunchbacked boy, had died before him.

Hangings in Glasgow during 'Buffy' McArthur's time were carried out at the Jail at the Cross, where 22 prisoners were executed between 1788 and 1813. Thereafter they were carried out at the front of the New Jail, in which Thomas Young resided.

The scaffold was not a permanent structure, for we find in one report of an execution performed in 1819:

"Tuesday night shortly after eleven, the materials of the scaffold were brought in front of the gaol, and the gallows erected. It was a fine moon-light night, and there was a very considerable concourse of people present; all was still, save the dull sound of the hammer and the occasional direct-ions uttered by the workmen to each other. Perhaps the greater part of the crowd consisted of females, and a number of them very well dressed."

The executions at this time took place in the afternoon, with Young wearing a blue coat with yellow buttons and scarlet collar. This was the Glasgow hangman's official costume, the use of which was restored by Young after being discontinued by McArthur — perhaps on account of the latter's unusual figure. On one occasion in 1819 a long drop was used:

"The unhappy prisoner Robertson mounted the scaffold with a firm step and a calm countenance. The drop was very considerable, and the crash excited a strong sensation throughout the surrounding multit-ude, not less, it is supposed, than 30,000; but it was his own request, as, from his being a light man, he was afraid of struggling."

In 1820 there was an execution for high treason. *The Gentleman's Magazine* (1820), II, 268-9, records it as follows:

" Aug.30   At Glasgow J.Wilson, convicted for high treason, was executed in front of the New Gaol.

The prisoner, when he came on the platform, was loudly cheered by the mob, as he was when he fell, with loud cries of "Murder!" and hisses. He fell at three o' clock, and was much convulsed. While hanging, blood appeared at his ears through the cap. At half-past three he was taken down, and the head was cut off, the body lying on the coffin. The man in the mask was saluted by hisses and cries of "Murder!" The head was cut off at one blow, and held up as usual."

Though Young carried out the hanging, he was not the man in the mask.

A few days after the death of Wilson, two men were similarly executed at Stirling. Young carried out the hangings, and this time both prisoners died without a struggle. There was, once again, a masked man whose part in the executions was received with hisses and cries of "Murder!"

"He appeared to be the same person who officiated at Glasgow, but he completely lost his former firmness and dexterity. He felt the neck of Hardie's corpse with his right hand, raised his ponderous hatchet, hesitated, lowered it, adjusted the crape on his face, and raised it again, and after two powerful strokes, a third slight touch was still necessary to sever some of the adhering fibres and skin. He then held up the head in the right hand to the shuddering spectators, and exclaimed, "This is the head of a traitor."

"He next turned round to the corpse of Baird, and took his aim apparently with less trepidation: the first stroke the axe cut the neck slightly and stuck fast in the wood, but the second severed the head from the body. He then held it up also, streaming with blood, and made the same proclamation, "this is the head of a traitor," and retired."

In 1816 Young assisted and instructed the newly-appointed hangman of Edinburgh, John Simpson, at the execution of John Black, who had been convicted of highway robbery.

In 1819, after Simpson had been dismissed from his post, Young carried out an execution there himself. He also performed his duties in Greenock, Paisley, Ayr and, possibly, Dumfries.

An obituary notice in *The Scots Times* says of him:

"When called to 'do business' in any of the surrounding towns, Thomas claimed very high fees; and, besides, made it part of his bargain to be driven to and from the place in a carriage, attended by a companion. When such instances occurred, he was lavish in his expenditure - lived in the best style - despised common liquors - drank wine and brandy, and treated his friends liberally."

He had some difficulty obtaining money due to him for the execution of Hardie and Baird, as we know from a holograph letter of 13th November, 1820, to the Town Clerk in Stirling. Whether he carried out later executions in Stirling we do not know.

On 11th May, 1825, Young was called upon to inflict a public whipping on John Kean, who had shot and wounded a fellow cotton-spinner. The sentence was carried out on a temporary scaffold in front of the court-house, the prisoner being bound to "an upright frame-work... as if extended on a cross".

It was said that associates of John Kean had collected £100 to bribe the hangman to avoid severity, but that he had been "kept out of the way" the previous day to prevent his being approached with it.

"The feelings of the multitude were, generally speaking, decidedly against the cold-blooded assassin," said *The Edinburgh Observer*. "The feeble hiss of disapprobation at the executioner when performing his duty, was drowned by the stronger expressions of regret that the punishment was not severer, and by the cheers which escaped the lips of numbers, when blood began to make its appearance on the back of the criminal."

Young, during his first ten years as hangman, had frequently whipped prisoners inside the jail, but he inflicted only two public whippings during the whole of his tenure of office. And in the case of John Kean *The Edinburgh Observer* commented:

"The executioner... seemed to do all he could, but the same nerve and knowledge which are sufficient to hang a man may be very unable to flog him, which fact, it is to be regretted, was overlooked on this occasion. Our magistrates, however, could not help themselves. They were bound by the strict letter of the sentence, and could employ no other person but the executioner, certainly neither a Samson nor a Hercules in his line."

After the whipping the criminal was conducted back to his cell to await the rest of his sentence– "banishment for life, and to be confined at hard labour on the public works, we presume at Bermuda, amongst other atrocious and hardened criminals".

Shortly afterwards Thomas Young was "violently assaulted and well flogged by a party of fellows in the Humane Society House, where, at their request, he had gone to partake of a glass of ginger- beer".

It was the only act of violence to which he is known to have been subjected.

Young, like Archibald McArthur, was an inoffensive fellow, and he was as regular - or almost as regular - in his habits as his employers could have wished. He had a wife and three children and was known to be a dog-lover. If, during his later years, he took to "the use of ardent spirits", he was by no means a drunkard.

He was fond of talking about his work and, when drinking, "seemed to take a strange delight in minutely describing the means by which any wretch coming under his hands might be promptly disposed of".

During his last years he was also weak from old age. The magistrates could no longer rely upon him to carry out his duties and retained an unemployed baker named John Murdoch as his assistant or deputy.

He died in the house where he resided on 9th November, 1837, leaving his family destitute.

The Persistent Hangman

On 23rd November, 1816, the magistrates of Edinburgh appointed John Simpson to be their hangman "in the room of John High deceased", with wages of 12s. a week and an allowance of 2s. a week for house-rent and taxes. He carried out his first execution on 11th December, assisted and instructed by his "brother functionary" from Glasgow, and his appointment was confirmed by the Town Council on the following 5th March.

He had previously served for several years in the Navy and, like Thomas Young, was able to furnish impressive character references at the time of his application for the post. In this he was undoubtedly seen as an improvement upon John High (commonly called Jock Heich), who is said to have accepted the post in 1784 (though his appointment is not recorded in the council minutes) in order to avoid punishment for stealing poultry. Even so, he was to remain hangman for little more than two years before being dismissed.

Simpson seems to have been a particularly unlucky hangman. On the very day that his appointment was confirmed by the Council he had the task of exposing John Morris, or Morrison, a perjurer, in the pillory. *The Edinburgh Evening Courant* the following day printed:

"*After the public executioner had performed* .

the duty of fastening the criminal to a machine
(bearing no resemblance to a pillory), he took his
post beside it; before he descended from the platform, much disapprobation was shown by the crowd,
which was speedily followed by showers of mud,
pieces of ice, sticks, stones, &c., being thrown at him
[the executioner].

"The unoffending object of their vengeance
bore this barbarous treatment with great patience,
and maintained his post with astonishing fortitude, till
the space, feebly attempted to be kept by the old
city guard, was broke in upon.

"The poor fellow was then treated with the
most wanton cruelty, - knocked down, - trampled on,
- kicked, and struck by every hand that could reach
him; even the audacious-looking villain, then undergoing the just sentence of the law, for a heinous
crime, presumed to kick the persecuted man, when he
was driven within his reach by the mob; he was also
observed, early in the tumult, to kick at the face of
one of the city guard.

"The executioner was at length delivered from
his savage persecutors by four respectable persons,
who succeeded in getting him into a stair, the
entrance to which they defended at imminent
personal danger.

"A strong body of the police arrived *after* this
stage of the disgraceful scene - but their services
were then of no use."

The item concluded: "We learn this morning,
that John Simpson, the executioner, remains extreme-
ly ill from the bruises he received in the above-
mentioned scandalous proceeding."

A further paragraph concerning the incident,
published in the same newspaper two days later,
stated that "the police establishment, in remaining at
the office till called for, acted upon that occasion in
strict conformity to orders officially communicated to
them."

It is not known how long Simpson remained ill

after being attacked, but, it did not prevent his continuing as hangman.

At the execution of Robert Johnston, a robber, on 30th December, 1818, there was an even more serious disturbance. This time it was caused by Simpson's own performance and led to his dismissal.

The execution took place on a scaffold with a collapsible platform in the Lawnmarket, in front of the New County Hall. Johnston, aged 22 and an old offender, mounted the scaffold with alacrity, looked round boldly and helped the hangman to adjust the halter, but the rope proved to be too long. When the platform was lowered the criminal's toes continued to touch it. The *Caledonian Mercury's* account states:

"A loud shout of horror, with cries of "murder", burst from an immense multitude assembled, and instantly a shower of stones thrown by persons in the crowd compelled the Magistrates and peace officers to abandon their stations, and no one but the criminal remained upon the scaffold; the Magistrates, clergymen, &c. being under the necessity of retiring into the porch of the Tolbooth church, adjacent to the Writers' Library; and from thence, through the aisle of the High Church, into the Police Office.

"Another cry of "Cut him down – he is alive," succeeded; and a person, genteely dressed, sprung upon the platform, cut the rope, and the culprit fell down in a reclining position upon the scaffold, after having hung about five minutes."

A riot ensued. Some of the people involved lifted the prisoner, removed the rope and cap and, finding that he was indeed still alive, carried him off towards the High Street. Others smashed windows of the church, stoned the police and tried unsuccessfully to demolish the scaffold. John Simpson, being in the hands of the rioters, "suffered severely".

"In the mean time the police officers rallied in augmented force, and retook the criminal from the mob, at the head of Advocates' close, carrying him

into the Police Office adjacent, where he was
immediately attended by the surgeon belonging to the
establishment, and bled in both arms, and in the
temporal vein, by which the half-suspended animation
was restored; but the unfortunate man did not utter
a word."

The bleeding was a mistake, as was soon to be
shown. For when order was restored - with the use
of soldiers from the Castle - the criminal was
carried back to the scaffold to be hanged again.

Simpson, who had evidently not been as badly
battered as at the pillorying of John Morris, carried
out his duty in the same bungling manner as before:
the condemned, having been 'turned off' a second
time, had now to be lifted in order that the rope
could be shortened with a few turns round the hook
by which it was attached to the overhead beam.

"Another shout of "murder", and "shame,
shame", broke from the crowd; but the place was
now well guarded with soldiers; and fortunately no
[further] outrage was attempted.

"Johnston was observed to struggle very much;
but his sufferings were at an end in a few minutes.

"The soldiers, who behaved throughout with the
utmost propriety, remained on the spot until the body
was cut down; and as it was then about dusk, the
crowd gradually dispersed."

John Simpson was dismissed from his post the
following morning, and one imagines that he left
Edinburgh without delay. Despite his experiences, he
was unwilling or unable to turn his back upon his
calling. He settled in Perth, apparently under the
name of John Foster, and obtained the post of hangman there.

He died of typhus in the town jail in late
October or early November the same year.

A 2nd Miscellany

The Sunday Times of 5th January, 1834, contains a report from *The Inverness Courier* saying that the post of hangman of that town had been abolished and giving details of the emoluments which the last occupant had enjoyed, in addition to his salary of £16 a year. The list is of extraordinary length:

"First, he was provided with a house, bed and bedding.

"Second, he was allowed 36 peats weekly from the tacksman of the petty customs.

"Third, he had a bushel of coals out of every cargo of English coals imported into the town.

"Fourth, he was allowed a piece of coal, as large as he could carry, out of every cargo of Scotch coals.

"Fifth, he had a peck of oatmeal out of every hundred bolls landed at the shore.

"Sixth, he had a fish from every creel or basket of fish brought to the market.

"Seventh, he had a penny for every sack of oatmeal sold at the market.

"Eighth, he had a peck of salt out of every cargo.

"Ninth, he was allowed every year a suit of clothes, two shirts, two pair of stockings, a hat, and two pair of shoes.

"Added to these fixed and regular sources of

income, [he] levied black mail on the lieges in the shape of Christmas boxes, and had besides a sum of 5 l.at every execution at which he presided."

The hangman in question, Donald Ross, had been appointed in 1812 and, during the course of his 21 or 22 years in office, had carried out only three executions.

The report adds that, taking all his emoluments into account, those three executions must each have cost the town nearly £400.

In 1770-1 the hangman of Aberdeen, whose name is unknown to us, was paid a salary of 6s.8d. per month, together with 15s. a year for his house-rent and £2.14s. for clothes.

On 30th December, 1773, Robert Welsh, newly appointed, petitioned for an increase in salary and the Town Council raised it to 13s.4d. a month. He was still in office in 1800-1, when his total income from the town was £12.7s. In 1803-4 he was succeeded by John McDonald, who died about the end of March, 1805.

The next Aberdeen hangman, John Milne, was appointed in April, 1806, when he was paid £7.10s. for six months' salary. He was still in office in 1818-9, when his total income was £19. This is all that is known of him.

The hangman's salary was increased to £25 a year in 1822, and remained that until 27th January, 1834, when the Town Council abolished the post.*

A report in *The Aberdeen Journal* of 1st July, 1788, shows that the town was not slow to use the collapsible platform once this device had been employed at Newgate:

"On Friday last, James Grant was hanged here in pursuance of his sentence at last circuit, for shop-

*Information from the Council Register and Burgh Accounts, supplied by Office of the Town Clerk & Chief Executive

breaking. He was executed in the way now used in England; a scaffold being erected in front of the prison, over which the gibbet projected; the place on which the criminal stood was made to fall down, and leave him suspended."

One of John Milne's victims, apparently, was John Barnet, alias McBarnet, who was hanged on 6th November, 1818, for housebreaking and theft. A report of his execution states:

"He died with great struggle; and, after hanging the usual time, the body was cut down, and conveyed, under the attending escort of the 88th regiment, to a boat ready to receive it, in which it was carried out, and sunk at sea."

In 1830 there occurred the execution of Catherine Davidson, alias Humphrey, for the murder of her husband. She was the first woman to be hanged in Aberdeen for 45 years. The hangman on this occasion was named Scott, and was said to be the assistant to the Edinburgh functionary. In all likelihood, it was John Scott, who is known to have been employed by the town and was later to be the hangman of Edinburgh himself.

In 1816 a Samuel Burrows was hangman of Chester: his name is mentioned in *The Lancaster Gazette* of 19th October that year, in a paragraph reproduced from a second newspaper, refuting statements made in a third.

The contentious item claimed that a public meeting had been held in Chester "to consider the present distresses of the country" and that at this meeting a certain clergyman had delivered a highly inflammatory speech. One of the other speakers was said to be "Mr. Samuel Burrows".

The paragraph refuting this report says that no such meeting had been convened; that some of the people who were reported to have taken part were "persons who, from their situations in life, would not be permitted to participate in proceedings of such respectability" and that the clergyman who was said to have been involved had been away from Chester on the day in question. "Mr.Samuel Burrows" was cited as one of the persons who would not have been allowed to take part in such proceedings.

Burrows is known to have carried out the execution of John Conner, for highway robbery, in Ruthin in 1824, and it is recorded that he had almost hanged himself the previous night during a demonstration of his methods.

On 15th September, 1830, he hanged William Griffith at Beaumaris for attempted murder, the prisoner putting up a desperate struggle when Burrows went to pinion him and continuing in this even to the extent of trying to displace the halter after it had been put round his neck.

This, however, is all the information that has come to light about Burrows.

On 2nd October, 1833, John Williams, hangman of Edinburgh, officiated at the execution of Robert Tennant, a murderer, in Stirling. He was an inexperienced hangman and, as he placed the rope in position, appears not to have noticed that the prisoner was wearing a neckcloth. To make things worse, Tennant was in a pathetic state, begging for mercy, while Williams awaited the signal to go ahead with his work. When the neckcloth was pointed out to him, the hangman went to remove it, but as he did so the signal was given and the prisoner was greatly agitated by the delay. This incensed the spectators, and we find in one report:

"As the executioner was proceeding through the Castlehill, on his return to Edinburgh, a crowd followed him till he reached some gardens near the bridge, in one of which he took shelter to escape the vengeance of the mob, who had become outrageous.

"They pursued him into the garden, where they got hold of him, and struck and abused him. Seeing his life in imminent peril, he made a desperate effort

to escape, and ran towards the river, followed by the crowd, who showered stones after him, several of which struck him.

"On reaching the river he plunged in, and swam towards the opposite side, where he was in great danger till the high constables arrived and drove off the crowd, and conveyed him to the gaol for safety."

Williams had been appointed to his post on 27th March that year, and had not yet carried out an execution in Edinburgh. He was not to do so, in fact, until 13th July, 1835, when he was called upon to hang James Bell, also for murder. And his performance then was to be even less satisfactory than it had been in Stirling.

Edinburgh's executions by this time were performed at the head of Libberton's Wynd, where a scaffold was erected as the need arose. On this occasion, the execution was watched by a very great number of people, many of whom were sympathetic towards the prisoner.

John Williams, on going to pinion him, "cried like a child, and made one or two abortive attempts before he could accomplish the task," says *The Edinburgh Evening Courant* of 16th July, but the reason for his "irresolution and incapacity" is not revealed. When the procession reached the scaffold a clergyman prayed for some time with the condemned.

Then the hangman suspended his rope, giving rise to yells and groans from the spectators - "expressions which the prisoner endeavoured to repress by turning round and beckoning with his hands", but there was worse to follow:

"The executioner... made one or two awkward attempts to adjust the rope, but not hitting the length, he tried to rectify his mistake, and was equally unsuccessful."

At this there were "loud and vehement cries of detestation... from all parts of the crowd" and the officials concerned, remembering the case of Robert

Johnston, were undoubtedly apprehensive.

"But, fortunately, at this critical period, Mr Brown, superintendent of public works, stepped forward, and with a firmness and presence of mind that does him the highest credit, pushed the executioner aside, and adjusted the rope to the scaffold with his own hand.

"The executioner then resumed his occupation, and placed the noose round the neck of the unfortunate culprit, who retained his wonted firmness during all this trying scene.

"This lamentable course of bungling, however, had not terminated, for when the culprit jerked aside the fatal signal with which the drop should have given away almost simultaneously, a few moments dreadful suspense occurred, during which the miserable victim shook with a sort of convulsive tremor, at the same time stretching out his hands in the attitude of prayer, as if to snatch the last moment of intercession.

"At last, however, the melancholy business terminated, and he died after one or two severe struggles."

Despite the bungling, there was no disorder. A large stone was thrown at the scaffold; others were thrown at the hangman by small boys as he left the scene - but that was all.

John Williams did not wait to be dismissed from his post: on 28th July it was reported to the council that he had moved out of the city with all his belongings, leaving the keys of the house allotted to him with a neighbour.

He had hanged only three people altogether: those in Stirling and Edinburgh and a third in Greenlaw. It is unlikely that he ever hanged anyone else.

A Hangman killed in the Street

Following the departure of John Williams, the Edinburgh Town Council appointed John Scott, "late Executioner at Aberdeen", to take his place. He was to hold office "during the pleasure of the Council only" - which is hardly surprising in view of the performance of his predecessor - but carried out an execution in Edinburgh a few days later without giving cause for complaint. He then went on to hold the post for the next 12 years.

His wages were 12s. a week, his fees 21s. for each execution and 10s.6d. for each whipping. He was also provided with a free house in the Old Fishmarket Close - the same house that had earlier been occupied by characters like John Dalgleish and John High. Additionally, he received £5 a year from the Court of Exchequer for serving as dempster. His income from the position must therefore have been a few pounds a year higher than it had been in Aberdeen - as, indeed, one would expect!

He was, of course, able to work elsewhere when he was not needed in Edinburgh. A report of the execution of William Perrie, a murderer, in Paisley in 1837 says:

"The Edinburgh executioner officiated on this occasion; and, from the manner in which he went about his duty, as well as from the complete and simple construction of the fatal apparatus, the

feelings of the crowd and of the prisoner were saved from all unnecessary torture."

After the death of Thomas Young, Edinburgh was the only authority in Scotland to have a hangman among its officials, though Glasgow paid a retainer to John Murdoch. The others simply engaged either Scott or Murdoch - generally the latter - when they needed a hangman, paying him fees and expenses.

In Edinburgh it was the custom at this time - or was to become so during Scott's tenure of office - for the hangman to be confined in the jail, at the expense of the city, for 8 days prior to an execution. This was to ensure his attendance and, no doubt, to guard against the danger of his getting drunk before carrying out his duty.

Even so, Scott's performance was not always to the satisfaction of his employers. At the execution of a tinker named Wemyss, in 1840, the condemned gave the signal for the hangman to finish his work, but the execution did not go according to plan, as *The Caledonian Mercury* report shows:

"An awful pause ensued - the executioner drew a bolt which turned out to be the wrong one. A groan of execration and hisses rose from the crowd. The executioner, evidently in desperation, tried by stamping with his heel to put the machinery of death in motion; but in vain.

"The commotion was increasing, when one of the officials in attendance ran up the steps of the scaffold and, withdrawing the bolt, an end was put to the agonies of the miserable man, and he was launched into eternity!"

Undoubtedly the magistrates were greatly displeased by this bungling, but not displeased enough, it seems, to dismiss the hangman from office.

John Scott, in fact, remained in the post until 12th August, 1847, when he was attacked and killed in the street near his home by an alcoholic named James Edie.

The crime, as reported in *Caledonian Mercury*

of 16th August, was unprovoked. Edie, described as "a broker and seller of watches", had been a member of the Edinburgh Total Abstinence Society for several years. He had, however, been "almost constantly under the influence of liquor" and given to outrageous conduct since violating his pledge four or five weeks earlier.

"On Thursday his behaviour was of a most violent character. Notwithstanding the exertions of some of his neighbours he proceeded up the Cowgate in an excited manner, threatening and assailing all he met.

"His attention was unfortunately directed towards a man of the name of John Scott, who was standing at the bottom of the old Fishmarket Close, and who, it is presumed, was obnoxious to Edie from the odium which attached to his profession, as being the common executioner for the city.

"After a brief altercation (though it is also said that no words were exchanged), Edie assaulted him in the most violent manner, knocking him down by repeated blows on the breast; and on Scott being carried to an adjoining shop, he was pursued thither by his assailant, who again struck him on the head, which produced immediate insensibility, and resulted in the death of Scott in a few minutes afterwards."

John Scott thus had the unenviable distinction of being, as far as we know, the only British hangman to die at the hands of an assailant.

"[He] had been for a long time past in a delicate state of health, which, it was supposed, had rendered the assault fatal; but, on a *post mortem* examination of the body on Friday by Dr Tait, we understand that the cause of death was found to be suffusion of the brain, the result of the blow which Scott had received on the head while in the shop.

"Edie was immediately taken into custody, and after an investigation of the case by the authorities, he was on Friday committed to take his trial for the offence."

A few days later the City Chamberlain formally reported Scott's death to the magistrates and council, telling them "that his Widow petitions to be permitted to occupy the dwelling house till the term of Whitsunday next". He also reported that he had paid the petitioner the wages that would have been due to her husband for the previous two weeks.

The council approved the Chamberlain's expenditure and agreed to allow the widow to remain in her house. At the same time it was decided that the vacancy created by Scott's death should not be filled.

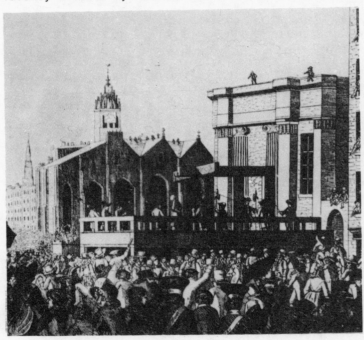

The scaffold in Edinburgh used for an execution in 1827.

The Octogenarian

John Murdoch was, as far as we know, the only
British hangman to continue working until he was
over 80 years of age. Yet, unlike most of our
subjects, he had no official post.

Born in 1767, he was a baker by trade, arriving
in Glasgow "from the north" in a state of poverty
about 1831, to seek employment of some sort from
the corporation. The magistrates paid him a retainer
to act as Thomas Young's assistant or deputy, and he
took to his new occupation without any qualms,
regarding the work as "perfectly necessary to good
government".

At Young's death in 1837 the magistrates
decided that they no longer needed a hangman among
their permanent officials, but continued to pay
Murdoch a retainer. He thereupon set himself up as a
peripatetic finisher of the law – if he had not done
so earlier – and for the next 14 years carried out
almost all of Scotland's executions outside Edinburgh,
as well as some in the north of England.

He is described in an obituary as being of
"stalwart form and grim visage (partially concealed
by an old high-necked waterproof)"; as taking a
pleasure in his work, and as holding "anything in the
shape of a reprieve or commutation in mortal
detestation".

As he became known to the populace of

Glasgow he ceased to live in the city "and took up his residence, sometimes in Paisley, sometimes in Kilmarnock, sometimes in the adjacent villages - such as Motherwell". On one occasion, it seems, he was found to be "officiating as a pastry-baker's assistant at one of our fashionable Clyde watering-places".

His obituary also tells us:

"The tidings of a murder case at a Glasgow Circuit always drew him forth. As soon as the Judges sat down, he reported his presence to the authorities, and then waited patiently in the hope that the man would be hanged. After sentence was pronounced he felt all right.

"That the mind of the Magistrates might be kept perfectly easy as to no accident taking place at the eleventh hour - for in this case, according to the old notion, the youngest Bailie must do the work - Old Murdoch always lodged himself in prison a week or ten days before the event, where he had bed and board at the public expense, and thus he was certain to be forthcoming when needed on the morning of the execution."

Among the executions carried out by Murdoch we find that of Dennis Doolan and Patrick Redding, who had murdered a railway ganger near Glasgow and were hanged in a field overlooking the scene of the crime. The event, which took place in 1841, was said to have caused "a prodigious sensation... exceeding that of any other execution that has probably ever taken place in Scotland". But the hangman himself seems not to have been moved by all the excitement:

"As Murdoch stood at the bottom of the scaffold immediately after the men had been thrown off, one of the authorities remarked that Doolan had not been properly handled, as he struggled and suffered much. "It's his ain fau't," said Murdoch, "nocht wad' ser' him but he wad tak' a jump when the drap gaed doon; but see, Sir, hoo kindly Redding's slippin' awa.""

In 1843 Allan Mair, aged 82, was hanged in Stirling for the murder of his "reputed wife", Mary Fletcher, aged 85. The hangman on this occasion was almost certainly Murdoch, but for some unknown reason he was "singularly attired in a light jacket and trousers, seamed with red and black, and a huge black crape mask." The prisoner was hanged sitting on a chair, as he was unable to stand.

A few months later Murdoch went to Edinburgh to hang James Bryce, who had murdered his brother-in-law; John Scott was presumably not able to undertake the task himself, perhaps through illness. Murdoch carried out his work there without mishap - as, indeed, he seems to have done almost everywhere else.

In 1849 a report of the execution of John Wilson, a railway labourer, in Jedburgh, stated:

"The executioner (Murdock of Glasgow), a feeble old man, and said to be upwards of 80 years old... adjusted the rope round [the prisoner's] neck, after which he handed the napkin to Wilson to give the signal when he wished the fatal bolt to be drawn.

"This was done almost immediately after it had been handed to him, and in an instant he was suspended in mid-air. Death must have been almost instantaneous, considering the depth he fell; and, as he scarcely gave a struggle, his agony must have been of brief duration."

And in a report of an execution in Glasgow early in 1850 we find:

"[Murdoch] is 82 years of age, and has a nerve like steel. Yesterday he had to mount the steps of the gallows by the help of a staff, but he did his duty with perfect coolness and composure."

He was by this time the only hangman left in Scotland and, in spite of suffering from rheumatism, readily travelled to Edinburgh to hang William Bennison, a wife-murderer, some months later. Apart from Glasgow, Stirling, Edinburgh and Jedburgh, he had carried out executions in Inverness, Aberdeen,

Ayr, Perth, Dundee, Newcastle and Carlisle.

His last known execution, that of Archibald Hare in Glasgow, was in October, 1851, when he was 84. Once again he "had to hirple after the criminal to the gallows by the aid of a staff", but "did his duty with nerves of steel" in spite of it. This time, however, the criminal only died "after a protracted struggle".

Thereafter, the magistrates of Glasgow turned to William Calcraft, the London hangman, when they needed somebody for an execution and Murdoch retired to the village of Bothwell. Being destitute, he was maintained by a monthly dole from the Glasgow Corporation, entered in the Chamberlain's Accounts as "criminal expenditure".

He died in Bothwell on 15th March, 1856.

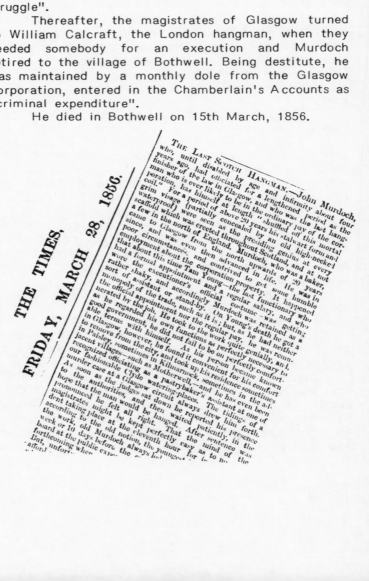

The Veteran Hangman

William Calcraft, having been appointed hangman of London in 1829, continued to hold his post until his enforced retirement in 1874. During the course of this extraordinarily long period of office his fame grew almost to rival that of Monmouth's executioner, even though the role of the hangman was by this time in decline. As a result of this, we have rather more literature concerning him than we have about any of his predecessors or "brother functionaries".

He was, in the first place, the subject - or, at least, the main subject - of a number of pamphlets and broadsides, the earliest of which, *The Groans of the Gallows* appeared in 1846. After his death in 1879, in addition to several newspaper obituaries, there appeared a full-length work, *The Life and Recollections of William Calcraft, the Hangman,* issued in 30 parts from the office of *The Illustrated Police News.*

Bearing in mind the dearth of publicity given to other hangmen, we can see that this was a rare distinction, especially as his personal life was comparatively uneventful. Unfortunately, this literature contains few biographical facts and much fiction and has, therefore, to be used with caution here.

It appears that Calcraft was born in Essex in 1800, though the exact location of his birthplace is

unknown. The *Life and Recollections* tells us that
he was a native of Chelmsford, *The Daily Telegraph*
of 17th December, 1879, that he was born in "a
small and pleasantly rural village". Both these
sources, such as they are, lead us to believe that he
arrived in London before reaching adulthood.

At some stage he learnt the trade of a boot-
and shoemaker, which he continued to follow for
much of his life, in between carrying out executions,
but he is said to have been a watchman for a firm
of brewers immediately before entering the service of
the Corporation of London.

His selection by the Court of Aldermen was
reported in *Bell's Life in London* on 5th April,
1829, having taken place a few days earlier:

"There were two candidates for the vacant
situation – one named Calcraft, and the other named
Smith.

"Calcraft had upon an emergency performed
the office of hangman very creditably at Lincoln upon
two unfortunate men, who, as he mentioned in his
petition, *went off without a struggle.*

"The other candidate had also a powerful
recommendation, but still it was not considered an
adequate test of his abilities, inasmuch as it did not
prove that was qualified to *tie,* although he could
dispatch by a quicker process.

"His petition stated that he had been long in
the army, and had been always selected to shoot
those who were pronounced by the Court Martial,
deserving of death...

"The Aldermen considered that Calcraft's
claims were stronger than those of his military
opponent, & they accordingly elected the former...

"Calcraft is a man of decent appearance; he
was yesterday in attendance at the Court of Aldermen, waiting, we believe, to be sworn in."

The role of the hangman had begun to decline
long before Calcraft's time, and continued to do so
after his appointment. No noblemen were beheaded

after 1747; no one was burnt at the stake after 1789. Hanging, disembowelment and quartering gave way, first to hanging and decapitation, then to hanging in the normal way. The discontinuation of *peine forte et dure*, the pillory, branding and mutilation curtailed the hangman's work still further.

At the time of Calcraft's appointment he was still expected to carry out public whippings, but later he lost this duty as well, the only whippings then being performed inside prisons by prison officers. The hangman's work thus became finally confined to hanging.

The number of executions, having risen considerably since Brunskill's occupation of the post, began to fall again. There had been over 200 capital offences in 1826. Peel, as Home Secretary, removed over 100 of them; a few years later the total was reduced to 15. Then, in 1861, it was further reduced to four (murder, treason, piracy and arson in a dockyard), three of which remain capital offences to this day*. Since that time nobody has been hanged in Britain except for murder, treason or espionage.

But official returns show that the number of executions fell in advance of these great changes in the law. There were 98 people hanged in London and Middlesex in the three years 1819-21; 51 in 1822-4; 53 in 1825-7; 52 in 1828-30; 12 in 1831-3; none in 1834-6; 3 in 1837-9; 4 in 1840-2; and 5 in 1843-5. Similar reductions are shown in figures for the whole of England and Wales during the same period.

Calcraft, however, was seldom without work for long, for he had few contemporaries in the same line of business and was therefore able to extend his sphere of operations to towns where his predecessors would not have been needed.

In addition to the many executions he carried out at Newgate and Horsemonger Lane Jails, he is

*These figures do not include wartime military offences, such as espionage.

known to have officiated at least once in Aberdeen,
Aldershot, Aylesbury, Bedford, Brecon, Bristol, Bury
St Edmunds, Cambridge, Cardiff, Carlisle, Chatham,
Chelmsford, Chester, Chipstead, Derby, Devizes,
Dorchester, Dumfries, Durham, Edinburgh, Exeter,
Glasgow, Gloucester, Greenlaw, Ipswich, Lancaster,
Leicester, Lewes, Lincoln, Linlithgow, Liverpool,
Maidstone, Manchester, Monmouth, Northampton,
Norwich, Oxford, Perth, Reading, Salford, Shrewsbury,
Swansea, Taunton, Winchester and Worcester.

Reports in *The Times* from which this list has
been largely compiled, show, too, that in some of
these places, particularly Chelmsford, Exeter, Ipswich,
Liverpool and Maidstone, Calcraft carried out
executions on several different occasions.

Among the most notable criminals who died at
his hands at Newgate were Esther Hibner in 1829
(just 9 days after he was sworn into office) for the
murder of her female apprentice; John Bishop and
Thomas Williams in 1831 for murdering an Italian
boy; Francois Courvoisier, a Swiss butler, in 1840, for
the murder of Lord William Russell, his employer;
Franz Muller, a German, in 1864, for a murder committed in a railway carriage; and Michael Barrett, a
Fenian, in 1868, for his part in causing an explosion
at Clerkenwell Prison, in which 12 people were killed
and 120 injured.

Other famous criminals he hanged include
Frederick George Manning and his wife, Marie, at
Horsemonger Lane in 1849 for the murder of Marie's
lover; Dr E W Pritchard in Glasgow in 1865 for the
murder of his wife and mother-in-law; and Allen,
Larkin and O'Brien, also Fenians, in Salford in 1867
for the murder of a policeman.

Generally, during the first 20 or 30 years,
Calcraft worked alone, but during his later years we
find that he was often assisted by Robert Ricketts
Anderson, alias Evans, the 'Medical Executioner' of
Carmarthen, and occasionally by 'Smith of Dudley',
the Stafford hangman.

He was paid a guinea a week by the Corporation of London, and a retainer of £5.5s. a quarter by the County of Surrey. He also received a fee each time his services were required by either of these authorities. Additionally, at the beginning of his tenure of office, he had an allowance from the Corporation for whips and birch-rods, but this, presumably, stopped when his work became confined to hanging.

For the executions he carried out in other parts of the country he was paid fees and expenses only, the size of the fee in each case being subject to negotiation with the authority concerned. Generally, he was paid £10 for a single hanging, but sometimes he demanded a larger sum. As for his long-established right to the clothes of the condemned, it is believed that he did not usually claim it.

Calcraft's performance at the execution of Esther Hibner was exemplary. Stubborn and violent, the prisoner had to be confined in a strait-jacket and carried to the scaffold, but when she was hanged she "did not make a single struggle, and appeared to die almost instantaneously". Calcraft's employers undoubtedly felt that they had chosen well.

But there were to be shocking mishaps at some of Calcraft's executions, probably the worst of them occurring in the case of William Bousfield at Newgate in 1856.

Bousfield, who had killed his wife and 3 children, was ill and weak. Being apparently unable to stand, he was hanged sitting on a chair. Yet suddenly he found the strength to put up a desperate struggle for survival:

"The sound of the falling drop had scarcely passed away when there was a shriek from the crowd of "He is up again!" and, to the horror of every one, it was found that the prisoner by a powerful muscular effort had drawn himself up completely to the level of the drop, that both his feet were resting

upon the edge of it, and he was vainly endeavouring
to raise his hands to the rope.

"One of the officers immediately rushed upon
the scaffold, and pushed the wretched man's feet
from their hold, but in an instant, by a violent
effort, he threw himself to the other side, and again
succeeded in getting both his feet on the edge of the
drop.

"Calcraft, who had left the scaffold, imagining
that all was over, was called back; he seized the
wretched criminal, but it was with considerable
difficulty that he forced him from the scaffold, and
he was again suspended.

"The short relief the wretched man had obtained from the pressure of the rope by these desperate efforts had probably enabled him to respire,
and, to the astonishment and horror of all the spectators, he a third time succeeded in placing his feet
upon the platform, and again his hands vainly
attempted to reach the fatal cord.

"Calcraft and two or three other men then
again forced the wretched man's feet from their
hold, and his legs" were held down until the final
struggle was over."

Calcraft was a family man, living for at least
the last 30 years of his life in Hoxton, at one time
in Devizes Street, later in Poole Street. During the
time that he was hangman the custom by which he
was paid his wages over the prison gate was brought
to an end and he was allowed to go inside the prison
to collect them. In his old age he often turned up
there accompanied by one of his grandchildren.

Though very strong, he was simple-minded and
- according to one source - "far from prepossessing
in his personal appearance". It has also been said
that he was "much given to angling in the New
River, and a devoted rabbit fancier", and that at one
stage he had a pet pony, which followed him about
like a dog.

His *Daily Telegraph* obituary gives us the

impression that he was a taciturn fellow, "particularly with respect to matters touching his
profession".

Another tells us:

"He conducted himself in such a quiet and
unostentatious manner as to be considered by the
English populace "mysterious". He went to and from
his executions in as private a way and with as little
ceremony as possible, and his conduct in this respect
was attributed to his fear of the people, who he
believed hated and despised him on account of his
office."

Yet in a letter to *The Times* written a few
days after the execution of the Mannings, Charles
Dickens commented:

"Mr Calcraft, the hangman (of whom I have
some information in reference to this last occasion),
should be restrained in his unseemly briskness, in his
jokes, his oaths, and his brandy."

In 1873 Calcraft went to Dundee to carry out
an execution, but the prisoner was unexpectedly
reprieved. In a report of the visit we find:

"On Saturday [Calcraft] had several conversations with gentlemen who happened to visit the jail.
He entered very minutely into his experiences, stating
that he felt exceedingly pained when called upon to
perform the functions of his office. It had, he said,
afforded him much gratification to learn that the
unfortunate prisoner whom he had come to hang had
been respited."

Setting out on his return to London, he arrived
at the West Station and found it "quite beseiged" by
spectators.

"[He] did not, however, manifest the slightest
discomposure. He inquired of one or two bystanders
what the people wanted to see, and was told that he
was the object of their solicitation. Evidently anxious
that all should have the fullest opportunity of
inspecting him, after taking his seat in a second-class
carriage he rose to the window, and kept his head

out till the train left the station."

There were, however, occasions when he was unnerved by the receipt of threatening letters. When Bousfield was hanged - as the Court of Aldermen heard the following day - "the moment he had drawn the bolt [he] absolutely ran away". At the executions of the three Fenians and Michael Barrett he was more nervous than the condemned.

In March, 1850, Calcraft was summonsed by the parish officers of the Witham Union in Essex for neglecting and refusing to support his aged mother, Sarah Calcraft, an inmate of the workhouse in Hatfield Peveril. The case was heard at the Worship Street police court, beginning on 6th March, and reported in *The Times*.

Mr Shee, the Relieving Officer of the Union, told the Court that Calcraft's mother, aged 73, had been in the workhouse for a fortnight. She had only two sons, one of whom "was wandering about the country, without any fixed habitation, or any apparent means of affording her relief". The Board of Guardians, he said, had therefore decided to proceed against the hangman for his mother's maintenance, and, in accordance with his instructions, Shee had travelled to London the previous day and "repaired to the defendant's house in Devizes-street, Hoxton".

There he had found Calcraft in the working dress of a shoemaker, which he believed to be his ordinary occupation. When Mr Shee disclosed the reason for his visit "the defendant positively refused to comply with the requisition of the board." It had, in consequence, been necessary to take out a summons against him. Sarah Calcraft was not in court herself by reason of her "state of helpless debility", said Mr Shee.

The case was adjourned for a week, as there was nobody to give evidence of Calcraft's income.

On resumption, the Governor or Newgate Prison appeared to tell the court that Calcraft was paid a guinea a week for his services to the Corporation. He received the money every Saturday from the witness's own hand.

Calcraft had not arrived in court on time; the hearing proceeding in his absence. After the Governor had finished his evidence the magistrate directed that a warrant be issued for the hangman's arrest, but he appeared soon afterwards, while the case was still in progress.

Sarah Calcraft was also there and gave evidence against him, remaining seated throughout the examination. She was 74 and totally destitute and so had been "constrained... to throw herself upon the parish," she said.

"Previous to that she had been sheltered for two years by her married daughter at Hatfield, with whom, upon entering the workhouse, she had left the few trifling articles that had not already been sold to supply her immediate wants; and before that had addressed three letters to the defendant, whom she had not seen for about three years, requesting assistance. but she had not received anything from him, and he had not even answered one of her communications.

"She had only one other child, a son, but he had been brought up to no regular employment, was sometimes in service, and generally jobbed about the country, earning a shilling in any manner he could.

"The defendant, she believed, was in circum-stances to support her, as, in addition to the salary he received from the corporation, he had another business, and carried on the trade of a boot and shoe maker."

The hangman was then asked if he could give any reasonable grounds for refusing to contribute towards his mother's maintenance.

"Defendant. - Well, I should be very happy to support her if it was in my power, but it is not; and as to what she says about the profits I derive from my shoemaking business, I can assure you that I have not earned a penny at that for a great number of

weeks.

"I have sustained a very severe personal injury – in fact, you never saw such an arm as I have got; I can neither get my coat on nor off without assistance; and, after being confined to my bed with it for more than two months, had a doctor's bill sent in to me for 10l.3s.6d., which I am totally incapable of paying at present, and he must wait for it.

"I admit that I receive a guinea a week from the city, but that is all we have to live upon, and when you deduct out of that 4s.6d. for rent, and the cost of a Sunday's dinner, you will find that there is not much left.

"It is not from want of feeling that I don't support my mother; she was in much better circumstances than I am; she had a large quantity of good furniture, and a number of silver spoons, and I can't see why she applied to the workhouse people at all."

The magistrate asked the hangman if he had any children to support.

"Yes, I have got three of them," he replied.

"How old are they?"

"As old as you are."

"Then, if that is the case, they cannot be much of a burden to you?"

"No, but they come sometimes, and, of course, put me to some expense extra."

"Well, you are clearly liable for the support of your mother, which is rendered imperative by an act as old as the reign of Elizabeth, and I feel it my duty to make an order upon you for the sum of three shillings per week."

"Ah, but you'll never get it from me!" said Calcraft. "I can't pay it, and, if you do, I must run in debt, I suppose."

"I shall make an order upon you for the sum of three shillings per week for your mother's support as long as she continues chargeable to the union workhouse, together with the costs attendant upon the present proceedings against you."

"Oh, very well! You may make your order if you like, but it's wholly out of my power."

Mr Shee told the court that his expenses amounted to £1.9s.6d., and the magistrate agreed that this sum would be included in the order. The hangman then turned to Mr Shee. "Well, now, suppose I took my mother to keep myself, what would you allow me for her?" he asked sharply. "Come, that's the point! Certainly, if you allow me something for her, I may be able to get on, perhaps!"

Mr Shee said that he intended to adhere to the order, as he believed that the defendant's mother would prefer to remain in the workhouse.

"Oh, dear, yes!" said Sarah Calcraft. "I should not be alive a week in London, whereas I should be safe in the country, if they even left me upon the common. I prefer being in the workhouse, for I am very comfortable there."

The Times concluding its report of the case, tells us:

"The defendant thereupon leant over his mother, expressing his willingness to take care of her, and with much apparent feeling told her that he was very sorry she should have had to come there at all; and upon the order being made, and one of the officers coming forward to raise her out of her chair, the defendant pushed him aside, and, gently raising her, with his arm round her waist, carefully supported her out of the court.

"There was a striking contrast between his compensating tenderness towards his mother and his rough coarseness to everybody else."

The case had excited interest and the court was crowded with people who had come to see the defendant. It gave rise to a broadside, *Calcraft's Lament, or the Hangman in a Hobble.*

Nearly 20 years later Calcraft was the defendant in another case, this time before the county court in Taunton. It arose out of his visit to the town in August, 1867, when he hanged George

Britten, a farmer who had murdered his wife. While
there he had stayed at the County Inn, running up a
bill of 13s.9d., which he left unpaid.

Mr Sulley, the landlord, wrote to him in
London, demanding payment, but succeeded only in
eliciting this reply:

London, Sept. th28,
1869.

Sulley, i am quite a Shamed at your meanness
of sending me that open peace of paper to expose
me in that way to think that you want me to spend
2 or 3 pounds to com to your place to Pay you the
sum of 14s. wich i never had half of it will Swear if
i had you had half of it what did it coust me when
whe ware out together you never spent one halfpenny
and you to charge me that exorbant sum i suppose
you thought of fritening me but i was born too near
a wood to be fritened by an Owl the sum you
charged me the Sheriff ought to have setteled long
ago i have sent you the Beastley bit of paper you
sent me in an invelope not open as you sent it me
you can doo what you like with it as soon as it is
convnant i will send you a post offic order for the
over charge of 14s. with a check upon you for so
mean an action. WS-WC. i never was served Such a
mean action in all my life i never hat such a thing
in my house before

mean   mean.

Mr Sulley, having already waited two years for
his money, was not satisfied with this and, on taking
the case to court, asked for an order for immediate
payment. Calcraft, we learn, did not appear personally, but a letter from him was read to the court
"complaining that he was overcharged, especially as
he had 'stood treat' for the landlord". It was pointed
out by the registrar "that Calcraft's trade had been
bad of late". The judge therefore allowed him a
month to settle the debt.

Public executions had by this time been
abolished, the last one to be carried out in England

being that of Michael Barrett, but Calcraft continued to be a public figure - as did other hangmen to a lesser extent.

He was now frequently assisted by R R Anderson, an eccentric amateur with private means, who - by his own account - took part in executions "from humane motives".

Anderson was the son of Evan Evans, a Carmarthen attorney; he was born about 1816. Instead of entering the medical profession, for which he had been intended, he spent his time - and a lot of money - on a variety of pursuits, attending prize-fights and cock-fights in addition to advising and assisting at executions. To the inhabitants of Carmarthen he was a well-known character, known as 'Evans the Hangman'.

At some stage he changed his name to Anderson - the name of his maternal grandfather, Captain Roberts Anderson of the 20th Light Dragoons - but in Carmarthen he was to be 'Evans the Hangman' for the rest of his life. He was said to be "an inveterate litigant", who enjoyed legal actions - regardless of their cost - and a practical joker, who could terrify his victims by pretending to hang them.

He wrote letters to the Home Office on the subject of the death penalty, one of which was published in *The Times* on 21st December, 1875. In this he set out his objection to the employment of "ignorant, brutish persons whom the love of gain and notoriety prompts to apply for the performance of the office" of hangman and urged that executions should instead be carried out by prison officers. Of himself and his experiences he wrote:

"For upwards of 20 years I have, from humane motives, devoted my attention to executions, and have attended nearly all the principal ones that have taken place in this kingdom during that long period, giving my advice and assistance to the executioner, and in no single instance where I have been present has the slightest failure occurred or any unnecessary suffering

been caused the unfortunate culprit.

"In cases where I have occasionally acted alone
- in triple executions, for instance, as at Liverpool,
Glocester, &c., my plans have been completely
successful...

"My career has attracted the notice of the
Press, by which I have been styled "the Amateur",
"the Doctor", "the Medical Executioner", and other

by writers who assumed to know my personal
history...

"The taking part in this business has not been
from a mercenary, but from a humane motive; and it
has cost me a large amount of time and money, and
has been a source of annoyance to some of my best
friends.

"I, however, have persevered in what I felt to
be a humane course, and my efforts were appreciated
by one, at least, eminent prison philanthropist, the
late Mr Wright, whose portrait, in his acts of mercy,
now adorns the Council Chamber of the Guildhall."

Anderson, irrespective of his opinions about
"ignorant, brutish persons" being employed as hangmen, was a personal friend of Calcraft's and was to
be on friendly terms with later hangmen too. He was
undoubtedly serious in his desire to see the death
penalty - to which he was opposed in principle -
inflicted humanely, if it had to be inflicted at all,
though we may be sure that his dissolute and
prankish ways did not encourage others to acknowledge this. For his own part, Calcraft seems not to
have resented Anderson's advice and assistance.
Indeed, a letter to Anderson from the Governor of
Newgate, dated 11th May, 1874 - preserved in the
National Library of Wales - states:

"The Sheriffs are very desirous that Calcraft
should have some assistance at an execution fixed for
the 25th Inst. and Calcraft named you as the person
he wished to be with him, and unless I hear to the
contrary I shall expect to see you here on Saturday
the 23rd Inst. by 10 a.m."

The fact that Calcraft was willing, over a long period, to accept advice and assistance from somebody like Anderson should be sufficient to dispel the image of him, handed down to us by Horace Bleackley, as an "ignorant and obstinate old hangman" who choked his victims to death.

The execution to which the Governor of Newgate's letter referred, that of James Godwin, who had murdered his wife, was the last one at which Calcraft officiated.

Soon afterwards, "in consequence of his advanced age, it was notified to him that it would be better for him to resign, and he accordingly did so... but his salary was continued to him by the Corporation".

During his last five and a half years he was not a happy person. His wife, who was five years older than he, had died in 1870; their marriage had lasted 45 years. And, in spite of his pension, he did not like being unemployed. One of his obituaries tells us:

"He always appeared to consider that he was unfairly dealt with by being compelled to resign his position as executioner, and was repeatedly heard to say to those who were acquainted with him that he was as well able to perform his duty as ever he was."

The veteran of the scaffold finally died at his home in Poole Street, in his eightieth year, on 13th December, 1879.

The Last York Hangman

At the time of his appointment as hangman of York, Nathaniel Howard, the coal-porter, was a resident of the city, aged about 60. He carried out his first execution, that of James Bradsley, who had murdered his own father, on 11th April, 1840, "disguised in a prison dress".

Unlike his predecessors, he appears not to have committed any crime himself; there is, at any rate, no reference to him in the Calendars of Prisoners and Quarter Sessions Minute Books for the previous 20 years. His appointment, which had been made in haste following the escape of James Coates, was therefore a departure from local custom. So perhaps the prison dress was a form of compromise rather than an attempt to conceal his identity.

He was evidently less than whole-hearted in accepting the office, for it was reported that at Bradsley's execution he "appeared much affected both before and after the performance of his task." However, he remained in the post for the next 13 years.

There were not many executions in York by this time: just one a year, on average, if William Knipe's *Criminal Chronology of York Castle* (1867) is to be trusted. But Howard is known to have officiated at Newcastle upon Tyne in 1850 and may well have carried out the occasional hanging elsewhere. Even so, he was not a hangman of any significance, especially in comparison with Calcraft.

His last execution was that of Henry Dobson in York on 9th April, 1853, when he went about his work "somewhat tardily", showing that "from old age and infirmity, he was totally incapable to perform the duties of his responsible situation". He afterwards resigned or was dismissed from the post, dying on 22nd April at the age of 73.

Thomas Askern, the next and last hangman of York, was a much younger man, born about 1816. His appointment seems not to have taken place until 1856 and only then because Calcraft was not available to carry out the execution of William Dove, a celebrated criminal who had murdered his wife in Leeds.

It is said of him in *The Heroes of the Guillotine and Gallows* (1868) that he had had a career of "abject poverty, want of employment, ill-luck in almost every one of his undertakings, and a too-fast life whenever his chequered destiny placed money, in small sums at a time, within his power".

He was a prisoner in York Castle at the time of Dove's impending execution, not for a crime, as this source suggests, but for debt. He carried out the hanging competently enough, the condemned man dying "with scarcely a struggle", and no doubt obtained his own release upon agreeing to become the regular York hangman.

Accounts of later executions in that city say that he lived in Maltby, near Rotherham.

He stayed in office for at least 21 years and is known to have officiated in Leeds, Durham, Lincoln, Nottingham, Edinburgh and Dumfries, as well as in York. *The Times* of 29th December, 1868, said that he was "frequently retained on these sad occasions in the northern and midland counties".

Not all his executions were accomplished as competently as the first. When John Hannah was hanged on 27th December, 1856, the work was "not very satisfactorily executed", and there were "some protracted struggles" on the part of the victim. Such struggles took place on a number of other occasions.

At an execution in Durham in 1865 the rope broke, the prisoner falling 15 feet to the ground. There was then a long delay while preparations were made to hang him again. The mishap caused intense excitement among the assembled crowds, but the prisoner was "apparently none the worse for the fall" and "seemed anxious to give the executioner as little trouble as possible". At the second attempt "Askern performed his office with great celerity".

A similar incident occurred at Armley Jail, in Leeds, some years after the abolition of public executions. John Henry Johnson, a fent-dealer, aged 37, was hanged on 3rd April, 1877, a number of journalists being allowed to witness the proceedings. The rope used was an old one and unusually short: a report in *The Times* commented that "it seemed as if it was not intended to allow a greater drop for the sufferer's body than 4ft."

"Seizing a lever, Askern pushed it from him, the boards gave way, and it was supposed that the victim had fulfilled the law's demands. But not so yet; for the rope had snapped asunder, and the doomed man had fallen prone to the ground. It is impossible to describe the consternation that prevailed among the small group of spectators.

"The chaplain seemed to have the greatest presence of mind, and he called aloud, "Let us all pray for him," at the same time himself penetrating within the framework of the gallows, which was encased in black drapery. Johnson was heard groaning, and the governor directed a chair to be brought.

"While the chaplain was praying that faith and fortitude might be granted to the poor wretch during this horrible interval, search was made for another and surer rope."

A new and thicker rope was brought to the scaffold and the unfortunate prisoner hanged afresh, but even then it was five minutes before his convulsions ceased.

There was, by this time, an even lower frequency of executions in York than there had been in Howard's time. It seems, in fact, that there were only nine people hanged there during the period 1856-77, so there was no justification for the city to have a hangman of its own and, when the post finally became vacant, nobody was appointed to it.

We do not know exactly when this occurred. Johnson's was the last execution at which Askern is known to have officiated and when Vincent Knowles Walker was hanged in York in April the following year, the executioner was William Marwood, Calcraft's successor at Newgate. So perhaps Askern had resigned or been removed from office in the meantime.

If not, he could only have stayed for a few months longer, for it is known that he died in Maltby at the age of 62, on 6th December, 1878.

Smith of Dudley

George Smith, the Stafford hangman, appears to have been first mentioned by name in connection with the execution of William Palmer, the Rugeley poisoner, on 14th June, 1856. Little was known of him at the time and his Christian name was given erroneously as John. He was, however, recognised as the regular hangman of Stafford, for *The Staffordshire Advertiser* of 21st June reported:

"The man who officiated as executioner... has performed the office several times at Stafford, and hung Moore for the Ash Flatts murder. He is a large man, in advanced middle age, and wore a long white smockfrock."

Palmer's had been the first execution in Stafford for 3 years. Before the previous one – that of Charles Moore, on 9th April, 1853 – there had not been any for 8 years. Therefore, if George Smith had officiated "several times" in Stafford before he hanged Palmer, he must have been hangman at least 11 years earlier. And this does seem to have been so.

The *Life and Recollections of Calcraft* states:

"Smith met Palmer in Stafford Gaol several years before Palmer was hung, Smith being a prisoner there for neglecting to maintain his wife.

"It was during one of these imprisonments that he volunteered to hang one or two men condemned for a brutal murder while they were in the employ-

ment of Messrs. Pickford and Co."

If this is correct, then it must have been he who hanged James Owen and George Thomas (described as boatmen in the newspapers) in 1840, for the only other double execution in Stafford between 1838 and 1856 was that of two young colliers in 1845. His career, in that case, must have lasted 32 or 33 years.

He did not have an official post and it has been suggested that he was only employed in the first place because he was willing to accept a lower fee than Calcraft. Once established as the Stafford hangman, he soon began to find work elsewhere to increase his income.

A Chester newspaper, reporting an execution that took place there on 24th April, 1841, says that the executioner was "a tall, stout man, dressed in white barragon, a practitioner from Staffordshire", adding that he had officiated at an execution in Stafford earlier the same month.

He was later said to be the executioner of the Midland Counties, as well as an occasional assistant to Calcraft. One source says that during the course of his career he hanged nearly 60 people, of whom 3 were females. William Palmer was the only one of those victims whose fame has lasted.

George Smith was a resident of Oakham, near Dudley, and it appears from his death certificate that he was born about 1805. He was variously stated to be "a labouring man", a shoe maker, a cattle-dealer and a former cow-doctor, so perhaps he could turn his hand to different types of work. His death certificate tells us that he was an agricultural labourer. He lived in a cottage near the site now occupied by a public house called The Hangman's Tree and was the subject of many local legends. He was often referred to as 'Smith of Dudley'.

No contemporary source has come to light to confirm the statement that he had been in prison for failing to maintain his wife. We have, likewise, no means of corroborating a statement made by Robert Graves in *They Hanged My Saintly Billy* (an account of the life of Palmer), that he "once ran a race against time, almost naked, through Wednesbury town, being sent to jail immediately on accomplishing this feat".

Hangings in Stafford were carried out at the front of the jail, on a scaffold "looking somewhat like a huge cattle-truck with a platform and a stout cross-beam overhead". The same structure was used inside the jail after public executions had been abolished.

Palmer's was by no means the only hanging to cause intense excitement there. *The Staffordshire Advertiser* of 16th April, 1853, reporting Charles Moore's execution, tells us:

"*On Friday night a considerable number oτ persons arrived in Stafford, and lodgings near the jail, especially in houses commanding a view of the place of execution, were in high request.*

"*During all the hours of the night stragglers on foot and parties in every description of conveyance, incessantly poured in.*

"*About four o'clock on Saturday morning the more anxious of the spectators began to take up positions near the barricades erected across all the approaches to the prison about 20 yards from the principal entrance, in the front of which the 'drop' was erected.*

"*From that hour up to the time fixed for the execution - 8 o'clock - a continuous stream of spectators flowed from all quarters towards the jail.*

"*The early trains from the north and south of the county also brought large numbers: though the 'special train' from the south, which was heavily laden, arrived about a quarter of an hour after the execution, greatly to the disappointment of hundreds who had come expressly for the purpose of seeing it.*"

It was the same when George Jackson, a

former soldier, was hanged in 1857. Rain fell in torrents during the night, so that "the channels of the streets ran down with turbid streams", yet vehicles kept arriving from all directions. The hangman himself took refuge in The Greyhound Inn in the company of a man named Michael Crutchley, but both were ejected by policemen after another customer had complained about their abuse.

The rain was still falling when the condemned was taken out to the scaffold, struggling violently; the crowds were unwilling to miss the hanging just to avoid being drenched.

For the execution of William Collier, a young tenant-farmer, in 1866, two pieces of rope were joined together, though not securely enough, as an account published in *The Times* shows:

"The floor fell, but instead of the culprit's head being seen above the scaffold boarding it altogether disappeared. There was a cry, "The man's down!" "The rope's broken!"

"The powerful tug which resulted from the falling of the culprit through the scaffold floor had, in fact, been too much for the fastening by which the rope held to the beam. The intertwined threads became liberated, the knot slipped, and Collier fell to the ground.

"For an instant there was dismay both upon and below the scaffold. The executioner was for a moment bewildered. He ran down the steps and beneath the platform, and found Collier upon his feet, but leaning against the side of the boarding, the cap over his face and the rope round his neck. He seemed to be unconscious, and the hangman turned back again, not knowing what to do.

"A new rope, delivered to the prison belatedly the previous evening, was immediately brought to the scaffold in order that the prisoner could be hanged again.

"A second time did the halter sway to and fro, and again did the priest, turnkeys, culprit, and hang-

man appear in sight of the crowd. Their re-appear-
ance was the signal for an outburst of popular
indignation. The hoots and calls were repeated until
the drop again fell."

In Warwick, in 1860, Smith hanged Francis
Price for the murder of a servant in Birmingham. His
conduct then was unusually brusque; the prisoner was
hanged before he had had the chance to finish
praying. This caused a lot of offence and led to a
serious disturbance shortly afterwards. A Warwickshire
newspaper reported it as follows:

"It appears that... Smith, after receiving his
fee, proceeded to the Great Western Railway Station,
to return to West Bromwich, and that he was recognised by some of the people waiting for the cheap
train to Birmingham, due at 1.17 p.m. ...

"He stood on the edge of the platform, and a
strong fellow mounted the balustrade, jumped upon
him, and bore him down on to the line, to which
some twenty or thirty other men soon made their
way.

"The 12.50 goods train, which does not stop at
Warwick, had not arrived, and one or two other trains
were also due. Some of the ring-leaders threatened
to push the executioner under the engine when it
came up, whilst others vowed vengeance upon him for
drawing the bolt before Price had time to finish his
prayer, and one or two accused him of pulling the
culprit's legs.

"Affairs were looking very serious. Mr. Chilton,
the Station Master, told the people that whatever the
executioner had done they had no right to commit a
trespass on the company's line, and shouted out, "The
express is due!"

"During the alarm thus created, Smith was
removed from the mob to the up side of the station.
Mr. Chilton then placed him in the second-class
waiting-room, locked the door, and put the key in his
pocket. About 300 persons, chiefly from Birmingham,
continued to shout and make a great disturbance.

"The government train to London arrived about two o'clock, Smith was placed in one of the carriages, and sent off to Leamington. The government train to Birmingham meanwhile arrived, and by it the mob went away. Smith returned to West Bromwich by the train which left Leamington at 2.40 p.m."

Smith's conduct at executions was not normally objectionable, as far as we can make out; he seems to have been no worse in this respect than Calcraft or Askern. Nor was he any more of a bungler than either of them, for, while some of his victims were reported to have "struggled for several minutes" or to have "struggled convulsively", others appear to have died almost instantaneously.

"Smith of Dudley" is known to have acted as Calcraft's assistant on two occasions in Maidstone. The first was on 11th January, 1866, when a man named Southey was hanged; it was snowing that day and there was a fierce wind, so that no more than 500 people gathered to watch. The second was the occasion of England's first private execution, that of Thomas Wells, a railway porter, on 13th August, 1868.

A newspaper report of the latter describes Smith as "a tall, thin, wiry man, with a keen eye, with his cheeks and part of his forehead closely shaved, dressed in a velveteen shooting coat, loose trousers, and a billycock hat, and looking like an acrobat who had donned his private clothes over his professional costume".

Smith had only one execution in Stafford after Collier's: that of Christopher Edwards, a locksmith of Willenhall, who had killed his wife with a poker. He was hanged inside the jail on 13th August, 1872, dying from strangulation after an unusually long struggle. There was not to be another execution in the town until the end of 1874, by which time Smith was dead. It is, however, likely that he carried out one or two other executions elsewhere during the last two years of his life.

The *Life and Recollections of Calcraft* tells us that Smith died on 3rd July, 1874, aged 70, but this is not correct. His death certificate shows that he died on 3rd April that year, aged 69. How the discrepancy arose we do not know.

A search of the Dudley newspapers of this period has failed to produce an obituary of him, which is surprising in view of the fact that he was such a well-known figure there. He has, nonetheless, lived on in local legend to the present day, though much that is said of him is of doubtful authenticity.

Conclusion

These were just a few of the hangmen who officiated in England, Wales and Scotland during the days of public executions. There were a good many others about whom we know nothing at all.

None of them appears to have been rich. It is probable that some of the London hangmen of Tudor and Stuart times did very well for themselves over fairly long periods. It seems likely, too, that Calcraft, carrying out executions all over the country, was often better off than his pleas of poverty would suggest. But we have no reason to believe that any of them amassed fortunes.

Other members of the profession, in London as elsewhere, are known to have been very poor.

If the holders of the London post were the best-paid hangmen of all, they were also the most disreputable. Of those who were in office between 1534 and 1786, Cratwell, the Hangman with the Stump Leg, Pascha Rose and John Price all ended their own lives on the gallows. Gregory Brandon, William Marvell, John Thrift and Edward Dennis were all convicted of capital offences, too, though none of them was actually hanged. It is also possible that Richard Brandon, Edward Dunn and even Thomas Turlis were capital offenders who managed to avoid punishment for their crimes. Bearing in mind that we know the names - in some cases little more than the names – of very few other London hangmen during the same period, this would appear to have some statistical significance.

But it would be a mistake to infer from it that the hangman was *usually* a criminal. Taking the whole of England and Scotland into account – and excluding York, where it was the custom to appoint reprieved felons to the post – the number of hangmen who committed capital offences was, in fact, relatively small. In many cases, we may be sure, the hangman was an honest and inoffensive man, who believed in the efficacy of his work and prided himself on having an official post, but such men leave few traces.

The degree of disesteem in which the hangman was held varied and, no doubt, his own character was one of the factors which affected it, but it was by no means the most important one: the main factor was the size of his role. In general, it was when the work was at its most loathsome – in the frequency and variety of the tasks involved – that the hangman's public standing was at its lowest. And it was only then that he was more often than not a thief or a ruffian himself.

As his role declined and his contemporaries felt less of a need to absolve themselves of any personal responsibility for his actions, his public standing rose and our sheriffs and magistrates were better able to find honest men to carry out the work.

Of the occupants of the London post *after* 1786, none appears to have got into any serious trouble with the law at all.

It cannot be pretended that the profession was ever entirely respectable. Yet Calcraft, Askern and Smith, the last hangmen to carry out their work in public, were generally regarded as objects of curiosity rather than contempt. In all likelihood the abolition of public executions improved the hangman's standing further.

By this time, however, the days of the full-time hangman were drawing to a close. Calcraft and Smith both had other occupations besides hanging, as did William Marwood, Calcraft's successor. Later hangmen, with the notable exception of James Berry, were to depend almost entirely on other occupations for their livelihoods.

The fact that they were able to do so shows the extent to which society's attitude towards the hangman had changed.

BIBLIOGRAPHICAL SOURCES

1. EARLY HANGMEN. Sir Edward Coke: **The First Part of the Institutes of the Lawes of England** (4th ed., 1639), p.86. Thomas Blount: **Fragmenta Antiquitatis** (1784 ed.), pp.272-3. **Calendar of the Patent Rolls**, 29th March, 1446. **Miscellanea Genealogicala et Heraldica** (1874), p.203. Samuel Pegge: **Curialia Miscellanea** (1818), pp.331-348. Thomas Madox: **The History and Antiquities of the Exchequer** (2nd ed., 1769), pp.372-5. Mary Bateson: **Borough Customs** (1904-6), I, 73-6. Wriothesley's **Chronicle**, I, 84-5. **D.N.B.** (ref. **Anne Boleyn**). Hall's **Chronicle**, p.826. Francis Grose & Thomas Astle (editors): **Antiquarian Repertory** (1809), IV, 501-20. Machyn's **Diary**, p.109. **The Gentleman's Magazine**, 1731, p.178. **Calendar of Common Council Book, Newcastle, 1699-1718** [Tyne & Wear County Archives Dept., ref. 589/6]. **A List of Executions in Newcastle-upon-Tyne since 1306** [Tyne & Wear County Archives Dept.]. John Sykes & T Fordyce: **Local Records** (1866-76), I, 129. J S Fleming: **Old Nooks of Stirling**, (1898), pp.39-54. J D Marwick (editor): **Extracts from the Records of the Burgh of Glasgow, 1573-1642** (1876), pp.233-4.

2. FATHER AND SON. J Payne Collier: **The Athenaeum**, 6th Feb. 1847. E G O'Donoghue: **Bridewell Hospital** (1929), p.11 & Notes. John Cordy Jeaffreson (editor): **Middlesex County Records** (1886-92), II, xx-xxi, xvii. **Middlesex County Records: Calendar of Sessions Rolls, Sessions Registers and Gaol Delivery Registers** [typewritten] VI, 68, 82, 118; VIII, 54. William Le Hardy (editor): **Calendar to the Sessions Records (County of Middlesex)** (1935-41), II, 279, 305; III, 104-5, 329. **Calendar of State Papers (Domestic Series)** Jan. 1617. Edmund Gibson: Introduction to Camden's **Britannia** (1695 ed.). Sir Henry Ellis (editor): **Original Letters**, 2nd Series, III, 340-2. **D.N.B.** (ref. **Richard Brandon**). J G Muddiman: **Trial of King Charles the First** (1928), pp. 147-8, 167-83. **Thomason Tracts**, E.562 (24) [B.L.] Sir Henry Ellis (editor): **The Obituary of Richard Smyth** (1849), p.35.

3. THE ORIGINAL JACK KETCH. Jeaffreson, III, 264-5; IV, 299-

300. The Devil's Cabinet Broke Open (1658), p.40 [G.L.].
Rebels no Saints (1661), pp.82-3. The History of the Life of
Thomas Ellwood (1714), pp.191-2. A Narrative of the Apprehend-
ing, Commitment, Arraignment, Condemnation, and Execution of
John James (1662), p.26. Notes and Queries 2nd Series, XI,
445-8. The Tyburn Ghost (1678) [G.L.]. The Plotter's Ballad
(1678). Somers Tracts, VIII, 129-31; IX, 260-4. Alfred Marks:
Tyburn Tree: its History and Annals (1908), p.201. The Life
and Times of Anthony Wood, II 552-4; III, 177. Sir Edward
Parry: The Bloody Assize (1929), p.196. Burnet's History of My
Own Time II, 382-4. The Hatton Correspondence, II, 32. The
Apologie of John Ketch Esq. (1683). Laurence Echard: The Hist-
ory of England (1707-18), III, 741, 772-3. Autobiography of
Sir John Bramston (1845), pp.192-3. George Roberts: The Life,
Progresses, and Rebellion of James, Duke of Monmouth (1844),
II, 150-3. The Scotts of Buccleuch, I, 451-2. Evelyn's Diary
(de Beer edition), IV, 456. D.N.B. (ref. John Ketch).Registers
of St James, Clerkenwell, vol.5. Edward Hatton: A New View of
London (1708), I, 77. The Man of Destiny's Hard Fortune
(1679). Narcissus Luttrell: A Brief Historical Relation of
State Affairs, I, 353, 370. J G Muddiman: The Bloody Assizes
(1929), p.29. Middlesex County Records [typewritten], VIII,
126-7. A Pleasant Discourse by way of Dialogue, between the
Old and New Jack Catch (1686) [G.L.]. Calendar of State
Papers (Domestic Series) Jan. 1686 to May 1687, No.196. Old
Bailey Sessions Papers, 20th-22nd May, 1686.
4. HANGMEN WITH A PEDIGREE. Edinburgh Town Council Minutes
[kept by the City Archivist], 1st July 1681, 20th August 1684,
30th August 1700, 20th August 1701, 1st July 1702. Sir Walter
Scott (editor): Chronological Notes of Scottish Affairs
(1822), pp.22, 98-9, 233-6. Sir John Lauder: Historical Notices of Scotish Affairs (1848), I, 295-6; II, 552; also, The
Decisions of the Lords of Council and Session (1759-61), I,
169, 302. Thomas Lane Ormiston: The Ormistons of Teviotdale
(1951), pp.49-50 and pedigree no. 70. The Register of Interments in the Greyfriars Burying-Ground, Edinburgh, 1658-1700.
The Register of Marriages for the Parish of Edinburgh, 1595-
1700. The Post Man, 29th June-2nd July, 1700. The Flying Post,
6th-8th, 13th-15th, 17th-20th & 20th-22nd August, 1700. William Carstares: State-Papers and Letters (1774), pp.615-6.

Robert Chambers: **Scottish Executioners (Chambers's Edinburgh Journal**, 22nd Feb, 1834). **A Description of the Parish of Melrose** (1743), pp.61-2.
5. THE SAILOR, THE BLACKSMITH AND THE "BAILIFF'S FOLLOWER". **Court of Aldermen: Reports & Papers, 1705-6** [G.R.O.]. Horace Bleackley: **The Hangmen of England** (1929), pp.11-2, 25. **A Compleat Collection of Remarkable Tryals...** of the most Notorious Malefactors (1721), IV, 240-7. Captain Alexander Smith: **The Comical and Tragical History of the Lives and Adventures of the most Noted Bayliffs** (1723), pp.26-8. **Old Bailey Sessions Papers**, 7th-9th December 1709, 6th-8th December 1710, 23rd-26th April 1718, 14th-16th October 1719. **The History of the Press-yard** (1717), pp.8-9, 59-62. **The Weekly-Journal or Saturday's-Post**, 9th March 1716, 9th & 30th November 1717, 6th December 1717, 26th April 1718, 31st May 1718, 26th September 1719, 17th & 24th October 1719, 28th May 1720. **The Original Weekly Journal**, 24th-31st August 1717, 2nd-9th, 9th-16th & 16th-23rd November 1717, 7th-14th June 1718, 24th October 1719. **The Weekly Journal or British Gazetteer**, 7th June 1718. Peter Wilson Coldham: **English Convicts in Colonial America** (Polyanthos, New Orleans, 1974-6), I, 302.
6. "DICK ARNOLD" AND THE COMICAL FELLOW. Captain Alexander Smith: **Memoirs of the Life and Times of the Famous Jonathan Wild** (1726), pp.8-9, 19. **A Seasonable Hue and Cry after the Pretender** (1719). Horace Bleackley (editor): **The Trial of Jack Sheppard** (1933), p.204. **The Weekly Journal or British Gazetteer** (or **Read's Weekly Journal or British Gazetteer**), 18th April 1719, 4th & 11th May, 17th August 1728, 10th March 1733. **Mist's Weekly Journal**, 1st May 1725. Marks, pp.229-30, 235-6. **The London Journal**, 29th May 1725, 29th March 1729. **Select Trials at the Sessions-House in the Old-Bailey** (1742), II, 287, 332. **Gloucester Journal**, 20th August, 1728. **Bruce's Weekly Journal**, 30th August, 1728. **Company of Barber-Surgeons: Tradesmens and other Accounts, 1722-36** [G.L., ms. 5269/1]. **The Country Journal or the Craftsman**, 29th March 1729, 10th March, 28th April 1733. **The Universal Spectator and Weekly Journal**, 10th & 31st March, 5th May 1733. **The Gentleman's Magazine**, 1733, p.267. **The Hangmen of England**, p.66. **Old Bailey Sessions Papers**, 6th-11th September 1732 (nos. 86, 87 & 88). **The British Journal**, 15th February, 29th March 1729, 21st February

1729(-30). **The Daily Courant**, 11th June 1731. **The Old Whig**, 13th March 1735.

7. THE IMPULSIVE HANGMAN. Sidney Young: **Annals of the Barber-Surgeons** (1890), pp.358, 421. **The Hangmen of England**, p.72. **The General Evening Post**, 22nd-25th May, 24th-27th July 1736. **The Weekly Miscellany**, 29th May, 5th June 1736. **The Gentleman's Magazine**, 1738, p.659; 1740, p.570; 1746, pp.391-4; 1752, pp.240-1. **The London Evening-Post**, 18th-20th January 1743. **The Daily Gazetteer**, 26th January 1741. Mrs Katherine Thomson: **Memoirs of the Jacobites** (1845-6), III, 447-8. **Old Bailey Sessions Papers**, 29th June-1st July 1743, 25th-30th April 1750. **Read's Weekly Journal or British Gazetteer**, 12th & 26th May, 2nd June 1750. **Old England**, 4th August 1750, 22nd September 1750, 23rd May 1752. **The General Advertiser**, 25th & 28th September 1750. **The Penny London Post**, 15th-17th October 1750. **The London Daily Advertiser**, 14th May 1752. **The Covent-Garden Journal**, 16th May 1752.

8. THE LAST HANGMEN OF TYBURN. **The Covent-Garden Journal**, 16th May 1752. **Read's Weekly Journal or British-Gazetteer** 23rd May 1752. **Old Bailey Sessions Papers**, 25th-30th June 1752, 28th June 1780 & following days. **The Hangmen of England**, pp.94, 132. **The Gentleman's Magazine**, 1760, pp.235-6; 1771, p.141; 1780, p.343; 1783, p.990. **The St James's Chronicle**, 25th-27th August, 1763, 13th-15th June 1780. **The Public Advertiser**, 12th April 1771, 14th, 15th, 22nd & 25th July, 11th August 1780. **The London Chronicle**, 11th-13th April 1771, 1st-4th & 6th-8th July 1780, 26th-28th & 28th-31st July 1781. **Repertories of the Court of Aldermen, 1814-5** [G.R.O.], pp.510-1. **The London Courant**, 12th July 1780. **The Attic Miscellany** (1791), I, 166-7. **The Daily Universal Register**, 22nd & 27th November 1786.

9. A DUMFRIES HANGMAN AND HIS DUES. **Dumfries Town Council Minutes** [kept in the Dumfries Museum], 17th April 1758, 3rd December 1760, 14th January, 10th May 1782, 23rd August, 22nd September 1785, 16th December 1786, 16th January 1787, 14th & 20th December 1789. William McDowall: **History of Dumfries** (1867), pp.692-5. **Chambers's Edinburgh Journal**, 22nd February 1834.

10. A MISCELLANY. Robert Wodrow: **The History of the Sufferings of the Church of Scotland** (1721-2), I, 260 & Appendix no. 11. **Notes and Queries**, 14th Series, CLVII, 299. William Andrews:

Old-Time Punishments (1890), pp.214, 217. Gloucestershire
Notes and Queries, IV, 266-7. The Times, 25th December 1835,
29th June 1789. The Edinburgh Evening Courant, 4th July 1772.
The Aberdeen Journal, 8th June 1789. Stirling Town Council
Minutes [Central Regional Council Archives Dept., Stirling],
2nd February 1771. Stirling Burgh Accounts, 1789-90 [Council
Archives Dept.]. Edinburgh Town Council Minutes, 25th July
1722. The Scottish Antiquary, XII, 13-9, 25-9. The London
Journal, 9th August 1729. Northern Notes and Queries, I, 7.
The Gentleman's Magazine, 1746, p.325. Chambers's Edinburgh
Journal, 22nd February 1834. The Caledonian Mercury, 18th July
1748. Western Circuit Gaol Book [P.R.O., ref. ASSI 23/8, part
2). The General Evening Post, 13th-16th August 1785. The Daily
Universal Register, 21st July 1785.   Calendar of Treasury
Books and Papers, 8th June 1743, 9th April 1745. Court of
Great Sessions Minute Book [National Library of Wales], March
1769. Court of Great Sessions Gaol Files [N.L.W.], March 1769.
Lloyds Evening Post, 19th-21st June 1769.
11. BRUNSKILL AND HIS MATE. Repertories of the Court of Aldermen, 1814-5, pp.510-1; 1816-7, pp.368-71. The Hangmen of England, pp.139, 161. The Gentleman's Magazine, 1797, I, 520;
1807, I, 171. The Times, 30th January 1794, 22nd February
1803. Sir Leon Radzinowicz: A History of the English Criminal
Law and its Administration from 1751 (1948-68), I, 147. Sir
Richard Phillips: A Million of Facts (1832), pp.526-7. Notes
and Queries, 1st Series, XII, 293. The Morning Chronicle, 2nd
May 1820. Annual Register, 1814, pp.76-7. Bell's Weekly Messenger, 18th December 1814, 4th May 1817.
12. OLD NED. Joseph Hall: Lancaster Castle; its History and
Associations (1843), pp.55-6, 49-50. Lancaster Gazette, 4th
January 1806, 22nd & 29th March 1806, 12th December 1812. Calendar of Crown Prisoners [Lancaster Record Office], March
1806. Bishops' Transcripts, St Mary's Parish Church [Lancaster
Record Office], December 1812. The Morning Post, 11th April
1806. Cowdroy's Manchester Gazette and Weekly Advertiser, 19th
April 1806, 19th December 1812.
13. A MAN FROM THE HULKS. Calendar of Felons, York Assizes
[North Yorkshire County Library], 18th March, 13th July 1793,
18th July 1801, 18th July 1835. Assize Records [P.R.O.], ref.
44/108, 44/116, 41/10. The York Courant, 18th August 1800,
17th April 1821, 7th April 1836, 16th April 1840. The York

Herald, 7th, 14th & 21st March 1801, 8th September 1821. **The Yorkshire Gazette,** 21st April, 8th September 1821, 14th November 1835. William Knipe: **Criminal Chronology of York Castle** (1867), pp.139, 197. **General Gaol Delivery, York Assizes** [North Yorkshire County Library], 23rd July 1814, 11th March 1815. **The Times,** 24th April 1821. **Thirsk Burial Register** [North Yorksire County Archives Dept.], 10th March 1841.

14. THE COMING OF CALCRAFT. **Repertories of the Court of Aldermen, 1814-5,** pp.471-3; **1816-7,** pp.368-9; **1818-9,** pp.19-23, 350-2; **1823-4,** p.393; **1827-8,** pp.535-6; **1829-30,** pp.463-4. John Ackerson Erredge: **History of Brighthelmston** (1862), pp.335-6. **Morning Advertiser,** 7th October 1837. **The Times,** 16th February, 20th August 1829, 13th July 1830. **The Morning Chronicle,** 2nd May 1820. J Curtis: **An Authentic and Faithful History of the Mysterious Murder of Maria Marten** (1828), pp.301-2. **The Heroes of the Guillotine and Gallows** (1868). **Notes and Queries,** 2nd Series, XI, 314-6. **The Observer,** 5th April 1829. **Bell's Life in London,** 5th April 1829.

15. NEITHER A SAMSON NOR A HERCULES. **The Scots Times** (Glasgow), 11th November 1837. **Strathclyde Regional Archives** [Glasgow], ref. A2/1/3, pp.59-61. **The Glasgow Herald,** 26th March 1856. James Pagan (editor): **Glasgow, Past and Present** (1851-6), II, 152-5. **The Times,** 17th December 1816, 13th April, 9th November 1819, 17th May 1825. **Glasgow Courier,** 12th September 1820. **The Glasgow Herald,** 26th March 1856.

16. THE PERSISTENT HANGMAN. **Edinburgh Town Council Minutes,** 5th March 1817. **The Times,** 17th December 1816. **Bell's Weekly Messenger,** 8th November 1819. **Chambers's Edinburgh Journal,** 22nd February 1834. **The Edinburgh Evening Courant,** 6th & 8th March 1817. **Caledonian Mercury,** 31st December 1818, 2nd January 1819.

17. A SECOND MISCELLANY. **The Sunday Times,** 5th January 1834. **The Aberdeen Journal,** 1st July 1788. **Caledonian Mercury,** 9th November 1818, 11th October 1830. **The Times,** 13th October 1830, 8th October 1833. **The Lancaster Gazette,** 19th October 1816. Lewis Jones: **Jones' Handbook for Ruthin and Vicinity** (Ruthin, 1884), pp.20-1. **Chester Courant and Anglo-Welsh Gazette,** 21st September 1830. **Edinburgh Town Council Minutes,** 28th July 1835. **The Edinburgh Evening Courant,** 16th July 1835.

18. A HANGMAN KILLED IN THE STREET. **Edinburgh Town Council**

Minutes, 28th July 1835, 24th August 1847. **The Edinburgh Evening Courant,** 6th August 1835. **Caledonian Mercury,** 19th October 1837, 18th April 1840, 16th & 26th August 1847. **The Life & Recollections of William Calcraft** (1880), p.239.

19. THE OCTOGENARIAN. **The Glasgow Herald,** 1st February 1850. 26th March 1856. **The Times,** 19th May 1841, 8th April 1844, 29th October 1849, 20th August 1850, 28th October 1851. **Stirling Journal,** 6th October 1843.

20. THE VETERAN HANGMAN. **The Illustrated Police News,** 27th December 1879. **The Daily Telegraph,** 17th December 1879. Arthur Griffiths: **The Chronicles of Newgate** (1884), II, 272-3, 412-4. **Bell's Life in London,** 5th April 1829. **The Times,** 14th April 1829, 24th February 1842, 25th February 1846, 5th August 1847, 19th November 1849, 7th & 14th March 1850, 1st & 2nd April 1856, 13th January 1866, 30th August 1867, 9th September 1868, 26th May, 30th June 1874, 21st December 1875, 17th December 1879. **The Morning Advertiser,** 16th December 1879. **The Life & Recollections of William Calcraft** (1880), pp.3-4, 240. **New York Times,** 16th December 1879. **The Dundee Advertiser,** 29th April 1873. **The Heroes of the Guillotine and Gallows** (1868). **Pall Mall Gazette,** 21st & 23rd October 1869. **Western Mail,** 28th August 1901. **Ms.** 12357E [National Library of Wales], pp.1353, 1358. **Papers of Griffith E Owen** [N.L.W.] **The Illustrated London News,** 20th December 1879.

21. THE LAST YORK HANGMEN. William Knipe: **Criminal Chronology of York Castle** (1867), pp.198-243, 248. **The York Courant,** 16th April 1840. **The Times,** 26th August 1850, 10th January 1859, 2nd January 1860, 17th March 1865, 29th December 1868, 4th April 1877. **The York Herald,** 16th April 1853, 14th December 1878 (two separate paragraphs). Griffiths, II, 273. **The Heroes of the Guillotine and Gallows. The Hangmen of England,** p.237.

22. SMITH OF DUDLEY. **The Times,** 16th June 1856, 28th December 1864, 13th January, 28th March, 8th August 1866. **The Staffordshire Advertiser,** 3rd April 1841, 1st February 1845, 16th April 1853, 21st June 1856, 15th August 1857, 17th August 1872, 2nd January 1875. **Life & Recollections of Calcraft,** p.237. **The Heroes of the Guillotine and Gallows. The Chester Chronicle,** 30th April 1841. **Express and Star** (Wolverhampton) 16th July 1968. **Black Country Bugle,** April 1970. **The Warwick and Warwickshire Advertiser,** 25th August 1860.

Nottingham	149	Swansea	136
Oakham	153	Taunton	9,136,143
Oxford	20,136	Thirsk	98
Paisley	112,132,136	Tinwall	74
Preston	7	Warwick	156
Reading	136	West Bromwich	156
Romanby	95	Westruther	28
Romney	7	Wigtown	79
Rugeley	152	Willenhall	157
Salford	136	Winchester	136
Shrewsbury	85,136	Witham	140
Stafford	152f	Woolwich	96
Stirling	10,26,81,111,	Worcester	136
	112,122,131	York	9,95f,148f

ACKNOWLEDGEMENTS

In seeking information for this book I have had occasion to contact archivists and librarians in many parts of the country. Some were able to help me to a greater or lesser extent; others, as might be expected, did not have the information I required. I am grateful to all of them for consulting their records on my behalf and have particularly to thank the following -

For their help and guidance concerning various Scottish hangmen I am indebted to Mr Donald Galbraith, Deputy Keeper, and Miss Margaret Young, Assistant Keeper, of the Scottish Record Office, Edinburgh; to Dr Walter H Makey, Edinburgh City Archivist; to Mr G A Dixon, Assistant Archivist, Central Regional Council Archives Department, Stirling; to Mr David Lockwood, Curator of the Dumfries Museum; to Miss Judith Cripps, Archivist, City of Aberdeen District Council; to Mr Richard Dell, Principal Archivist, Strathclyde Regional Archives, Glasgow; and to the staff of thhe Glasgow Room of The Mitchell Library, Glasgow.

For their help wit English provincial hangmen I must thank Mr David Bromwich, Local History Librarian, Somerset Local History Library, Taunton; to the staff of the Somerset Record Office, Taunton, and in particular to Mr R J E Bush; to the staff of the North Yorkshire County Library, Reference & Information Library, York; to the staff of the Tyne & Wear County Council Archives Department, Newcastle upon Tyne; to Mr J Keith Bishop, Lancashire County Archivist; and to the staff of the Archives and Local History Department of Dudley Library.

I am similarly grateful to Mr W T Barnes, Senior Assistant Archivist, Department of Manuscripts & Records, National Library of Wales, and Mr A G Veysey, Clwyd County Archivist, for information about executions in Wales; and to Mr Richard E Huws of the Department of printed Books, National Library of Wales, for many items about R R Anderson, alias Evans.

I have made use of almost all the information obtained in this way, and hope that those who provided it will not be displeased by its presentation.

JAMES BLAND